THE
LEADERSHIP
REVOLUTION

Stairsteps Back to Simplicity

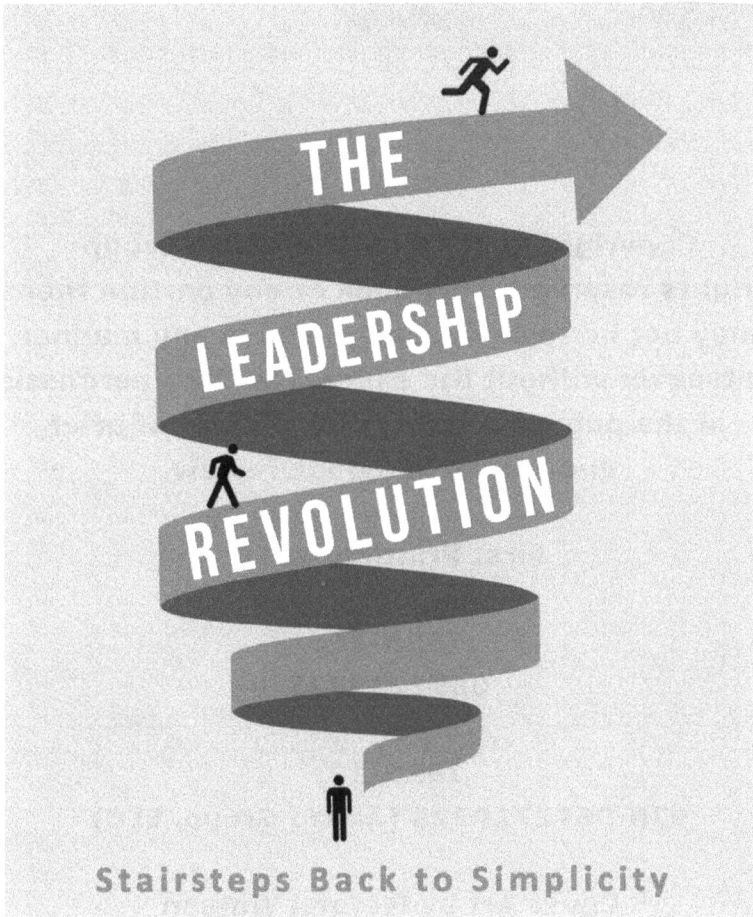

By The Allazo Group

Lead Author - Scott Catt

First Printing, 2016

ISBN-10:
0692719725

ISBN-13:
978-0692719725 (Allazo Group, LLC)

Cover Art by Morgan Watson

Allazo Group, LLC

Allazogroup.com

TABLE OF CONTENTS

Praise for the Leadership Revolution

"Leaders are made and the principles found in The Leadership Revolution will help anyone become one. These principles have stood the test of time and are applicable from startup to Fortune 500 Company. Scott Catt lays out the steps to becoming a leader in such a simple and interactive format that anyone at any level of the organization will benefit."

- Brandon Wright, CEO Giftry

"From c-level executives to young professionals, this book is a must read for anyone that's part of a team and wants to reach new levels of excellence. There are important lessons found in the Leadership Revolution that will help you on your quest towards the highest levels of leadership."

- Russell Ochoa, CMO, Avantar

The Leadership Revolution is exactly what I needed to simplify my leadership approach. It doesn't overwhelm with complicated frameworks, but instead offers concise applicable suggestions. All the examples are easily relatable no matter age or station. I responded to the emphasis on the cyclicality of leadership development and the learning process, which ebbs and flows. This book provides a rare glimpse into true growth.

- Carmen Fenn, MBA, Oxford University - Strategic Program Manager at Vivint, Inc.

There have been many books written on leadership and leadership development. Most of those focus on narrow approaches and actionable habits. Scott Catt focuses on the principles that drive good leadership, and by changing dogma and paradigm of what makes a leader, he inspires us to internalize its principles.

- Diogo Myrrha - Vice President, Stoneway Capital

"Become, Empower, Unite, and Elevate" – "everyone can be a leader." The Leadership Revolution is spot on in its assessment of leadership. Throughout my career and even my life, I've noticed that men and women of integrity and perspective can be an influence for good wherever they stand. As an educator, my focus is on the rising generation. We are raising our world's future leaders in our homes, schools and work places. We need a generation of leaders who strive to reach their full potential, and our committed to shaping our future for the better. I hope we can apply these principles within our own circles of influence. The ripple effect will be phenomenal!

- Michelle Evans, Renowned Educator and Thought Leader

Dedication

To Scott Foster who became more than a dozen of those city kids, Dick Catt who empowered the human race with love, Wayne Allen who unites man with charity and divinity and Frank Okoren who has elevated every man, woman, child, family or organization that has been blessed enough to cross his path.

Preface

This book has been a labor of love. It started as a simple conversation amongst young professionals years ago. The discussion was simple, "Why are there so many contradictions in leadership theory?" We took different classes from different professors and worked for an array of managers. We heard astonishingly different thoughts on what made a leader. This led to a challenge to take everything we heard, read and experienced and try to somehow boil it down into a simple formula in which explained the primary themes that tied the theories together. Our findings were the motivation for this book. The simplicity in leadership found in the following overarching principles can be discovered throughout time, and have proven advantageous to thousands upon thousands of leaders across the world, and across generations.

This book will walk you through crucial steps of understanding and living a life of leadership. A thesis of the entire book would be that development never ends; you are either moving up a metaphorical staircase or down it. You can't stand still. It starts with you. It starts with your thoughts, which will transform your life. Then, you are to transform others around you, culminating in uniting groups big and small. Then, you do it again, only with more innovation, passion, and commitment. It is truly an upward revolution. Sounds simple? Good. That's the idea. Sounds complicated? Take it one step at a time, both literally and figuratively.

The purpose of this book is to both teach and be a lasting resource of leadership development. Therefore, you will find many opportunities to reflect, answer questions, and create plans for improvement. The concepts are simple, but often forgotten. The process, however, is not the point. The point is to transform your actions by first transforming you; your thoughts, the way you see the world and the way you work with those around you. We invite you to take advantage of the interactive component of our book.

The journey behind this book has led us to countless interviews, mounds of research and a new understanding of our own personal leadership experiences. It has transformed us into better leaders ourselves. We are more knowledgeable, self-aware, and hopefully, more impactful. We hope for a similar journey for you and those within your massive sphere of influence, (which is MUCH bigger than you think). There is an old proverb that says, "Blessed is the leader who seeks the best for those he serves." There is another by Lao Tzu which reads, "Be gentle and you can be bold; be frugal and you can be liberal; avoid putting yourself before others and you can become a leader among men." We believe in both of these teachings.

We feel our research was unique in the aspect that the answers to our questions, and to your questions, didn't come from our own "war stories." They came from history, the successes of others, and a rigorous quest for simplicity, codifying complex leadership theory into universal and timeless principles. From there, we gave suggestions founded in common sense, thus came the sub title, "Stairsteps Back to Simplicity." We have found, what you have probably already found out for yourself, that it is easy to complicate leadership, but sometimes you have to work hard, and almost always, have to work smart to simplify leadership. Personal stories shared are the result of reflecting on these principles, not creating them.

There are several people we need to thank. Without them, this book would not have been possible. First, a huge thank you to Leanne Coleman and Peter Fuller for your brilliant insights and contributions. We express our gratitude to Tanner Shelton for his expertise and artistic abilities. Thank you to Katy Kempton and Andrew Miller, this work wouldn't be what it is without you. Thank you to Travis Catt, MSW, for putting complex issues into a beautiful style grounded in simplicity, and to Tammy Foster for her encouragement and brilliance. Lastly, to Kord Catt for his diligence and leadership and to Mark, a giant among men, who has set the pace by never stopping his run up the stairs of leadership, and we need to thank those leaders who we have met, and those who we have only met through history, for their insights, lives, and commitment to excellence. We hope this book honors them.

Lastly, we invite you to use this work as a springboard. As mentioned before, this book is meant to be a lasting resource. You can read it once with one view and another time from a completely different vantage point. You can read it cover to cover or in the sections you feel most applicable to your situation. Fill out the workbook sections, drink liberally from its concepts, and think deeply on the principles. As your life and leadership progress, your views will change and you should take the time to record those new illuminations. They will prove invaluable. Leadership is found in action. For example, taking a step upwards on a staircase will lead to previously unseen vistas. By turning the page, you are taking that first step, and with that first step, the Revolution of Leadership begins.

- The Allazo Group

INTRODUCTION

You'll find that our book departs from the vast majority of current leadership material in its inclusivity of **everyone** under the umbrella of "leader." To become a leader, you need no specific pedigree. There is no specific checklist of talents that every leader must innately have, nor is leadership limited to those of a specific age, title, gender, or industry. Leaders aren't only those to whom masses of employees answer, or to whom eloquent public speaking comes naturally. In short, leadership isn't an arcane science, mastered only by Abraham Lincoln and the Dalai Lama; almost anyone in any capacity can become a leader, and that includes you!

We're not going to babble about any "golden approaches" to powerful leadership, nor will we profess to have the quick and easy steps to becoming a veritable George Washington. Leadership books with empty promises are a dime a dozen. Instead, we're going to focus on the foundational principles of leadership, the nuts and bolts that are applicable to absolutely everyone. When we understand the core framework on which leadership should be viewed, all of the particulars come into focus.

Our job is to break down and explain the framework and steps of what we call "The Leadership Revolution"; your job is in practical application. As you read, you'll come to understand the four steps of the Revolution: what you can become, how you can empower others, how to unite those around you, and how you elevate or enhance the process, making the next round of the revolution more effective. Become, Empower, Unite, and Elevate. You will come to know these principles well.

We know that storytelling can illustrate principles more clearly than simple explanations. Here's a couple of stories that can help you understand the process of becoming, empowering, uniting and elevating.

Moses and Leadership

Whether you're a fan of the Bible or not, the story of Moses is fascinating. Born a Hebrew slave, he was saved as an infant by a mother who put him in a wicker basket and set him afloat down the world's longest river. Miraculously, he was found by Pharaoh's daughter, who raised him as her own. Brought up in luxury but with an eye for justice, Moses killed a man he found beating a Hebrew slave to death. Forced to flee his land, Moses left behind the trappings of royalty and a position in Pharaoh's court. For a time thereafter, he lived a life of solitude as a shepherd in the wilderness. His chance to be Pharaoh was squandered; the leadership boat had seemingly passed Moses by.

However, fate had other plans. As he tended his flocks in the wilderness, he was given divine direction by way of a burning bush. His task? Leave the sheep behind, return to Egypt and free his entire nation from bondage. He would have to become a man worthy to be the leader of a historic nation, with enough courage to face down the Pharaoh of Egypt and enough mettle to lead a stubborn Israelite nation to its promised land. This was no small task for a shepherd! Born a Hebrew slave, he was to become the quintessential leader of his time.

Moses, unrelenting but untried, fulfilled his commission. He confronted Pharaoh no less than ten times, astonished the masses with plagues and calamities, organized a mass exodus, caused the Red Sea to part and defeated the great Egyptian army. And may we mention that he was not the most elegant of speakers as he did all of this?

He led his people through the wilderness, guided them by divine intervention to food and water, and established the Ten Commandments, which are still the founding moral principle of much of the world's population.

Let's pause for a second and relate this back to the Leadership Revolution. Moses couldn't have lead a nation out of bondage as a pampered prince, neither was it possible as a lonely shepherd. If he was going to cut it, he was going to have to go through the first step of **becoming** someone better. Let's look at a couple things he did to become someone more well equipped to free the Hebrews.

Observation 1: He acted in self-defense of a Hebrew slave who was being beat to death. Moses had the courage to stand up for what was right, even though he had every reason as a part of Pharaoh's court to turn his head the other way.

Observation 2: That first act of doing what was right didn't pay immediate dividends. Forced from his land, he became someone new. The life of a shepherd gave him years of wilderness reflection, where he thought about who he would become.

Observation 3: When the time was right and when he was ready, the opportunity presented itself to become a leader and he didn't question it. Moses confidently went back to Egypt. Ultimately, through his strength of mind and a newfound humility, he became a leader.

Moses didn't wake up and save a nation. He didn't just decide to stop the Red Sea with an army behind him, with muddy sandals and howling winds while holding back water that, if let go, meant certain death. He followed the path every leader must take, the path *he never thought* he would take.

Having come down from Mt. Sinai with the Ten Commandments, Moses sees a nation quick to complain and slow to progress. They were actually complaining about being brought out of captivity. No, seriously, they would rather be under the rule of Pharaoh than going to the promised land. What does Moses do? He attempts to change the culture and belief of his people. Not their religious belief, per se, but their belief in what they could accomplish, their belief in what they could become. He begins the Israelites on their 40-year sojourn through the wilderness, breaking down their bad habits and replacing them with patience, diligence and mutual trust. He begins to communicate powerfully through his brother Aaron, but there is no question who the real leader is. His example shouts louder than words.

This brings us to the 2nd step in the Leadership Revolution: **Empowering**. Moses knows that his path doesn't end with just becoming a leader himself, recognizing that lasting change will only come if he can pass on his positive changes to those around him.

Observation 4: Moses knew as well as anyone, that though he had come this far alone, he needed the talents and skills of others. Reuniting with his brother Aaron, who was strong in speech, was the first piece of the puzzle which allowed Moses to play to his strengths while empowering other leaders around him to play to theirs. Moses was able to gain a powerful ally in leadership by empowering his brother. Aaron hadn't seen the burning bush or been apprised to the entire game plan, but he knew he had the confidence of Moses and acted honorably in that trust. Together, they would rally the Israelites, defeat the greatest army in the world, and set off on an adventure to the promised land with Moses as their leader.

Observation 5: Moses saw potential in his people, notwithstanding all of their whining. He recognized that they would never reach the promised land without his help. However, more importantly, he recognized that reaching the promised land by himself would be meaningless. Even if it took 40 years, he was going to unite the Israelite Nation together and facilitate lasting change.

Even with Aaron's help, the load of administration began to wear on Moses so much so that his father-in-law feared he might die of exhaustion. In a mark of powerful leadership, he changes the course of the nation by teaching Moses the strength found in empowering others and delegating responsibility. Moses should get credit for listening. Delegation happens, vision increases, and Moses is able to do more with less hours by prioritizing his time with the most important things put first.

The effectiveness of the Leadership Revolution is exponentially magnified by the 3rd step: **Uniting.** Leaders come in all shapes and sizes and serve in different positions. Working as a united front,

Observation 7: One person alone can't adequately lead. Moses's leadership became increasingly more powerful as he delegated it out to Aaron and other leaders.

In the end, the goal was to get to the Promised Land. Moses didn't take them there. The change that was needed for this people in bondage took longer than the life of their first leader even though he stayed committed to the goal until the very end. Luckily, Moses prepared other leaders, Joshua being the greatest among them. Joshua had internalized the vision and even though no one would *want* to be the leader to follow Moses, Joshua was ready.

In an epic speech, Joshua led the Israelites in a united front across the River Jordan into the promised land. He was a regular guy who learned from an extraordinary leader, only to become legendary in his own right. If it could happen to him, it can happen to anyone willing to take advantage of the opportunities presented to him.

To finish off the Leadership Revolution, Moses **elevates** the Israelites, taking them to a whole new epoch of success as a nation. Elevation in this sense can be defined as a paradigm shift. As the Leadership Revolution unfolds, you'll see positive growth and change culminating in a complete culture shift. No longer were the Israelites a petulant, lazy nation: they had become a strong, united, empowered nation, capable of marching into the promised land.

Observation 8: Through his leadership example, Moses elevated the Israelites onto a new plane of positive thinking. A leader recognizes when the fog of negative thinking and laziness have set into the people's collective mindset. By following the Leadership Revolution, Moses elevated them out of the fog and into a confident, positive mindset.

Observation 9: It turns out the path wasn't easy for Moses, and it hasn't been easy for most of the leaders who have walked the earth, offices, homes, or sidelines. Moses may have had the vision, but too many of the Israelites were lacking that vision. Moses rolled up his sleeves and got to work, showed us an unrelenting example of the Leadership Revolution facilitating lasting change throughout an entire nation.

For a different perspective, consider the following fictional story.

There was a young man who found himself in a large building with all the elevators out of order. This left a massive spiral staircase and as much initiative as he had to get to the top. With determination he took the first step upward. *Why do the elevators have to be out of order?* He asked himself. After one revolution around the staircase, he noticed the window on the second floor had a different view from the busy street of his city that he saw minutes before. After the second revolution around the staircase, his vantage point became more expansive. He could see more on the street from above than he ever could walking on it from below. By the fifth revolution, though tired, he looked out to see details of the city he had never noticed before. By the fifteenth revolution, he found a platform that had windows on all sides. The view stole his breath as he could clearly see the sunset in the west, lake in the east, and a spectacular view of the city from every other angle. The higher he climbed, passing one window on each side of the building as he went, his attitude towards the city changed. It wasn't just crowded, busy and full of unidentified people, it was something beautiful, complex and spectacular when viewed from a higher perspective.

This young man's climb up this spectacular staircase will match your climb to become a confident leader. There is no secret genetic makeup associated with a leader, just as there is no age, title, or industry. There is, however, an upward revolution you must take, step by step, view by view, by passing windows on all four sides of the building that allow you to see clearly four distinct vistas: what you must become, how you must empower others, how to unite

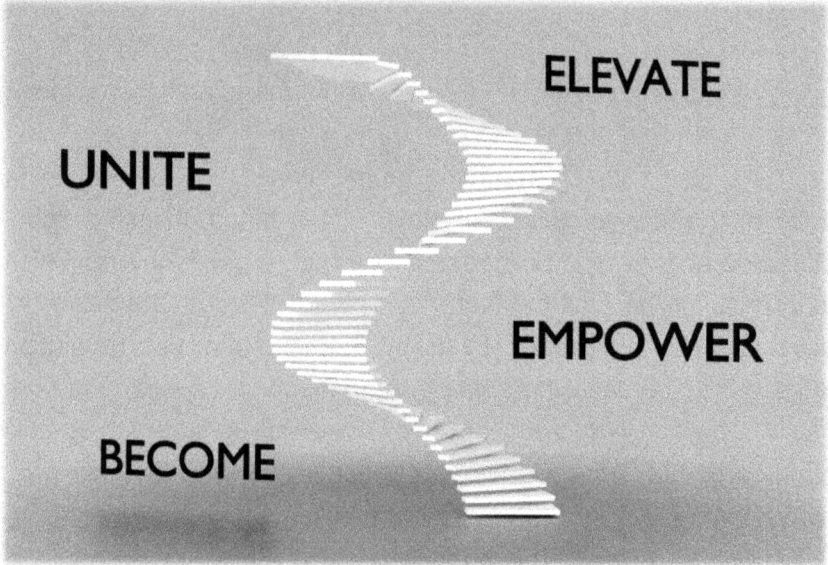

your team, and how you elevate or enhance the process, making the next round of the revolution more effective with a greater, clearer view. What are the four sides of the Revolution? Become, Empower, Unite, and Elevate. You've heard them before, now we want you to think of them... often. Remember, leadership is a verb and it starts in the mind.

The Purpose of This Book

The purpose of this book is simple. It is here to help you, and those around you, to reach their full potential in life and leadership. But if you are like most people who take the time to read books such as this, you may justifiably ask, "What makes your book different?," or perhaps, "Why should I trust you?". Both are great questions, and before we progress any further, they need to be answered.

First of all, why is our book different? With thousands of titles on countless shelves and sites across the world, it can be difficult to discern what really works in leadership from the mere hearsay. In our opinion, books on leadership and organizational theory have slowly drifted so incredibly far away from the central principles that they have become contradictory, combative, and even compulsive in their claims. Our goal in this book is to get back to basics and provide real, applicable principles which have stood the tests of time. It is safe to say that our aim is to lay the foundation on which you can build a reliable and sustainable leadership development plan for you and for those in your charge. Simplicity is our goal since what works is most often found in simplicity.

Secondly, why should you trust us? To put it simply, you don't need to trust us. The principles we teach within this book have stood the test of time. In reality, they were not written by us, but by thousands of the world's greatest leaders whose names are both known and unknown over countless generations. It would be wise to trust them. As executives, and in our interactions with others in an array of leadership positions, we discovered that no matter what the strategy may be, the underlying bedrock of leadership is always the same. It is a little known cycle that holds the secret of the staircase from a level of mediocrity to a level of being remarkable in your own leadership, and from average results to extraordinary results in leadership throughout just about any organization.

This book is not just about learning another way to lead, but about leading in what the greatest leaders in history would deem the right way. This book will not necessarily teach you to do more than you are already doing, but to take your current efforts and cultivate them in a way that maximizes results and efficiency. This book is simple in nature because at the heart of leadership, doing less efficiently is always better than doing more inefficiently. We must never mistake activity for productivity, and in the following pages, we will help you to know the difference. It never does one well to have a specific destination in mind with nothing but guesses on how to get there. In the words of the great American inventor Alexander Graham Bell, "The sun's rays do not burn until brought to a focus." We plan to focus your energies and passion on a path towards excellence.

We are not as concerned about "good approaches" to leadership (for they are a dime a dozen) as we are on the great principles of leadership. When we understand the framework on which leadership should be viewed, all of the particulars come into focus. This book is also unique in that it isn't just intended to be for your development as a leader, but the development of those around you. There is a lesson there, and it is our goal for this book to model the mindset we hope you choose to propagate. Everyone can be a leader.

Because this book is for everyone, you should expect to learn from everyone. There are names in the book of leaders you will recognize. There will also be names you don't recognize because they are "everyday people," not viewed by the public eye. At the same time, you should be learning from yourself as you reflect on the book and from others who you discuss the book with. Fame does not hold a direct correlation with leadership. We are more interested in the ideas of a junior high student council officer following the revolution than an egotistical CEO who is not.

So what is this cycle and why are we so confident in it? This book has evolved over years of conversations with some of the brightest minds the world has to offer, not only in business, but in the realms of psychology, education, statistics, families, and non profits, just to list a few. We are not inventors, for we simply took the existing truths weaved across the fabric of multi-disciplinary leadership success and put them into a codified, ready-to-use model. Ideally, you would buy this book this morning, and feel an exciting level of confidence in new skills and understanding by this evening. We want you to walk away with an increased excitement on what you already know and found to be highly successful in your leadership efforts. We hope that you come to the realization that if you are a confident leader, with the respect of your employees and those who have entrusted you to a leadership position, it is likely you will find within these pages that you are not too far off, and are probably applying many of these universal principles already. Keep in mind, our goal at The Allazo Group is about constant, upward, and empowering change, so we invite you to take what works and add to it in a meaningful way.

A disclaimer: There ARE many amazing books on leadership out there in circulation already. We would recommend those books, and those incredible thought leaders. Don't get the idea, in any way, that we are telling you that all of these books are wrong. Some, of course, are better than others, but we feel confident that our book falls squarely in the realm of "some" and not in "others." If our passion for this topic over took our sense of practicality, this book would be at least 10 volumes long. As such, we understand that we will not cover every topic and every discipline with the attention it deserves. However, we do promise that we will give you everything you need to lay a foundation for success, perfectly suited with the tools to build a legacy of leadership that is applicable and powerful to your situation, today and and in thirty years, no matter where your career takes you. It works, and if you apply the principles we teach, you will see for yourself. It will take diligence, an open mind, and an open heart, but what could be more rewarding? What could make more of an impact on your career?

The Cycle: Become, Empower, Unite, and Elevate

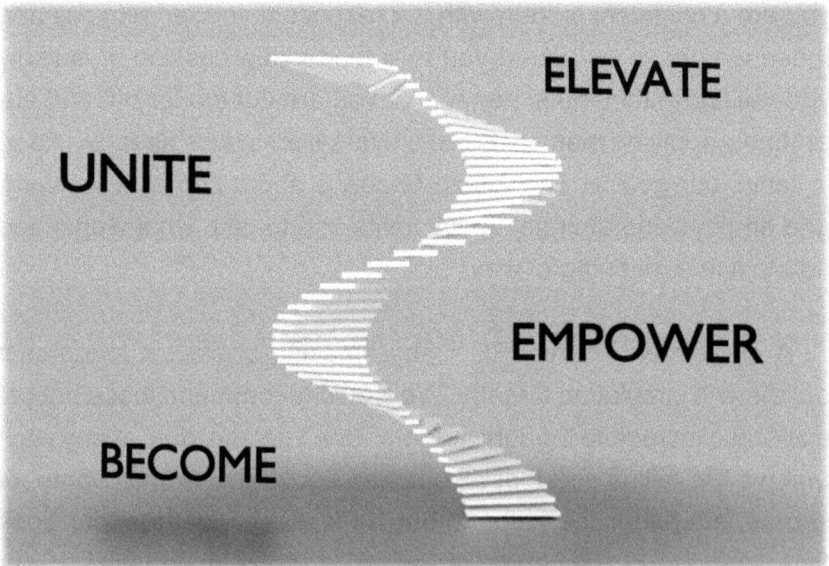

This cycle also helps to debunk several myths that have existed over generations on the subjects of leaders, leadership, and organizational theory. A few of the more important ones include:

Myth: Leaders are just born. You either are one, or you aren't.

Truth: There is no question that leadership takes skill, and that those skills can be acquired. Leaders are not just born. They are made. Through experience, the application of correct principles, and a high degree of self and organizational awareness, an average man or woman can become a life changing leader, and an established leader can become an astounding leader in her capacity for change. In fact, there are millions, if not more, of average people out there who are in leadership positions and don't even realize it. Our goal is to reach them in the process and help them to see their potential.

Myth: Management and leadership are the same thing.

Truth: Managerial skills are skills worth acquiring. In some ways, they may be complementary, but they are not the same skills it takes to be a leader. To connect them too closely is a quick path to leadership failure. So much has been already written on the topic, but it would be sufficient to say that managers have people who clock in every day to "go to work," while leaders have people who follow them because they choose to. Because they want to. Our focus in this book is to help you become a leader and not another manager.

Myth: Your positional status within an organization is the strongest indication of your true effectiveness as a leader.

Truth: The best organizations quickly learn that leadership exists at all levels of the organization. Without harnessing the power of an all-hands-on-deck leadership approach, with everyone feeling empowered towards the organization's goals, you will quickly find your team underachieving, under engaged, and under committed to long term growth.

Myth: You need people reporting to you to be a real leader.

Truth: Some of the greatest leaders we know are those who lead themselves to excellence. Leadership often means leading who you are now to the person you want to become. Additionally, we have seen many leaders, without a single person reporting to them, greatly influence organizational outcomes purely from their example and from the influence they have through personal relationships with their peers. Is this not the definition of a true leader?

Myth: If you're not a Grade A extrovert, you're not a leader.

Truth: It comes back to what was said before; example and personal interest in one-on-one settings are two of the most powerful forms of leadership. When examining Abraham Lincoln, Eleanor Roosevelt, Gandhi, and Rosa Parks, we could ask the question, what do they all have in common? They were all leaders who changed the world, and by all accounts, they were introverts. The myth that you must be naturally outgoing to be a leader needs to be put to rest, because it did not stop any of the four leaders listed above from reaching their full leadership potential and it doesn't need to stop anyone today.

The Leadership Revolution is built upon principles that apply to every leader, no matter what his age, position, or experience. When mastered, it can unlock the greatness in human potential.

THE CYCLE

A Revolution Back to Simplicity

We, like so many others, believe in this cycle. It is simple, yet profound. It can be applied by the youngest of our students to the most seasoned of our CEO's. If you picked up this book, you are on a journey to highly effective leadership, and we are honored to give you a breakdown of the following roadmap that will get you there again and again.

1. **Become.** By design, the cycle really begins and ends with YOU; your decisions, your desire to learn, your implementation of career changing principles, and what you want out of life. Our life and our leadership are undoubtedly connected. At the end of the day, who we are will always shine brighter than what we do.

Charles Du Bos, the noted French critic, once made the point, "The important thing is this: to be able at any moment to sacrifice what we are for what we could become." What you can become is a far more efficient and impactful leader than you ever thought possible. Once you are a leader (and as said, chances are you already are one), it is your responsibility to become what you must become to make the greatest difference throughout your organization. We will teach you the reason and the why behind this, and if you will use this book as a workbook, it will also go a long way in teaching you not only what attributes and competencies making that difference entails, but how to make them a part of your life as well.

2. **Empower:** To empower others and to guide them to greatness is one of the most noble and admirable of human qualities. It is a real gift that some naturally possess, but one everyone can

develop. Really, it is in that moment when we look outside ourselves and start looking at the people around us as people; people with real talents and abilities, people with real challenges and concerns, people with real potential to not only make a difference in your organization, but in the world. Harnessing this power is one of the greatest forces of good at a leader's disposal.

A wise person whose name has since been lost to the depths of history once said, "Leaders instill in their people a hope for success and a belief in themselves. Positive leaders empower people to accomplish their goals." This is the mandate to every leader, and the second step in the Leadership Revolution. Once you become what you need to become, it is your duty to help others become what they need to become. Always remember that it's not the other way around! It begins with you.

3. **Unite:** A key part of empowering is also inspiring individuals to believe in and buy into the organization's mission and purpose. Once that takes place, you will find yourself on the third step of the revolution; uniting your team. In a mechanic's shop, when you have assembled every part of an engine, that engine is ready to be used to propel a car. The same imagery works here; everyone does his part in harmony to propel the organization forward on the road to higher success.

Aristotle was once cited in declaring, "In union there is strength." It is in disunity that we find weakness. It is in disunity that we find great individual team members operating under the facade that there was never a team at all. The strength of your organization can be measured by the unity of your people. It is easy to cut down a twig but much harder to ground an oak tree. As you unite your team towards a common purpose, don't be surprised when things you never thought possible start to happen.

4. **Elevate:** The fourth step of the revolution is the most overlooked step, which is why it is also the most crucial to consider. This step is employed by the greatest leaders while it is ignored, or not even conceived, by the masses. It is the step that will take you back to the first step of the next floor, completing the revolution and allowing yourself to begin again as a higher level leader with a higher level team.

To magnify or elevate an item or individual means to increase the importance or effect of that item or individual; or, in other words, to enlarge, enhance, maximize, expand, or intensify. So if you are going to elevate the leadership process, you are going to enhance your leadership capabilities, maximize the strength of the individuals in your organization by continually empowering them, expanding your unity to touch all parts of the organization, and then do it again at a higher level, enlarging your influence and the influence of others exponentially.

This Revolution is simple and it is powerful. When understood, it changes lives and organizations. Sticking with the cycle and making it a part of everything you do is crucial. You may not be there yet, but by committing to following the teachings of this book, you are closer than you were yesterday. So if you are ready, let's take the next step, the first step on the revolution upward. Let us learn together the power behind becoming.

BECOMING

You Need to Be Something Before Accomplishing Great Things

If you are reading this book, we are making a couple of assumptions; first is that you are, in one way or another, a leader. You may not believe it yet, but that's ok. We do. In the words of President John Quincy Adams, "If your actions inspire others to dream more, learn more, do more and become more, you are a leader." These "others" can be found in your organizations, your family, your friends, your classmates, and in many cases, your better self.

Our second assumption is that you don't want to be an average leader (even if you don't think you are a leader at all yet) but have a strong desire to become a great leader. The kind that changes lives and organizations. If these are true, keep reading. If they aren't true, keep reading. You will want to by the end.

There is an old saying, "To gain something you've never had, you need to do things you've never done." We'll take this logic even further by considering these two questions. What if the quote continued? Would it make a difference? "In order to do things you've never done, you must become something you've never been." It makes all the difference in the world.

It's an interesting thought but a powerful principle when viewed in the context of leadership. There are times in life where doing simple, normal things will help you to become better at a task. For example, there are some members of the Allazo Group that are excellent golfers, there is another one who is... well, not good because he had never really tried. So he goes out, buys the gear, buys the clubs, golf balls, the whole nine. At this point, with tee time in hand, he had technically become a golfer, but not a good one. His first time on the green was a complete disaster. By definition, he had become a golfer, but no one would believe it if they saw him. The verb "to become", over and over, is the real power behind becoming. For example, he first had to become effective at even placing the golf ball on the tee, then become effective in his swing, then driving followed by his short game, strategy and on and on. There is no luck when you are becoming, it is simply to become something and then another thing and then another thing until you have ACTUALLY become something. In this case, this man will eventually "become" a golfer. It's not luck. It's a mindset and a process. It brings to life the idea that the harder you work, the "luckier" you get.

So really, we could just as easily say that in order to gain more confidence as a golfer, the kind of golfer only the ambitious strive for, you must actually become something in the process. You don't wake up as a talented golfer. You start the process of becoming the golfer you aspire to be. You take that gift you may or may not have, and systematically cultivate it through the process by working to become exceptional at one thing and then another, focusing on the end goal along the way. By doing so, you become so much more, a student of the game, a master of the course, a vessel for learning, and a prepared guide for others preparing to find relaxation on the back nine.

If your goal is to golf, there isn't much to do, go and buy a club and show up to the public course. If you want to be a world class golfer, there is not only more to do, but that constant state of becoming. The promise here is that it is achievable! This is the power to be harnessed when we really understand the concept of becoming.

This power not only applies in our personal lives and in things such as golfing, but in the organizations we lead, regardless of size or industry; families, churches, Fortune 500's, school teams, it doesn't matter. We have heard the stories of incredible feats, the naturals that walk in and take this or that by storm and accomplish something great without much real effort at all. But how often does that really work out? Not often, and definitely not enough to bank on it when your destiny is on the line. Those stories are circumstantial. Real leadership is situational. Preparation is key to lasting success.

Let's try an activity:

I want you to think about the three most successful leaders you know.

You can measure "successful leadership" in any way you'd like. Your yardstick of success could be a religious leader who is a powerful orator, a mother who skillfully balances career and family, or a business leader who manages to reach out to employees of every level. It might be helpful to do this activity several times with several different definitions of "successful leadership" that are meaningful to YOU. These definitions of "successful leadership" will likely be the bedrock of what you wish to emulate.

First, in no particular order, name them and number them, visualizing what successes you see in their leadership today. Now, I want you to think about their lives. How did they become the successful leaders they are in your eyes? What steps, sacrifices, and resources helped them in their journey? Be as specific as possible. Ask them or ask others if needed. Write as much as you can think of. Chances are they didn't just wake up and find the "leadership success" they have now.

Let's take this fictional story as a case study.

Example 1: John Jones, a powerful leader in my community who has inspired hundreds to action. John started out in a rough family and had every reason to fail if he chose to. Instead, he left home at fifteen to get away from those rough influences. He became a straight A student and got a full scholarship to the local university. Instead of attending parties, he attended chamber of commerce meetings and other community events. He made connections and worked his plans out with people he respected in order to create a position for himself to where he could help youth in a similar situation to him. He sacrificed higher paying jobs out of college in order to work in community development. After work, he continued to mentor youth, volunteering and making valuable connections that eventually helped him start his own nonprofit organization. He gained so much respect in the community that soon enough, a scholarship that he helped fundraise was allocated to give underprivileged kids each year a chance to study at the same local university he attended. He was elected to the town council and still continues his passion by learning, growing, and coming up with more and more innovative ways to help youth.

Activity 1: _____

_____

_____

_____

_____

Now for each of those successful leaders, take out three or four of the steps you recognized as key reasons for their success today. What do you think their life would look like today without those key components? Same process; name them and number them and answer the question with as much detail as you can.

Example 2: John Jones: If he had never made the decision to leave home at such a young age to live with relatives, he still likely would have found a way to succeed but his life would have looked a lot different. He likely would not have gotten the grades he needed for that full ride scholarship and that would have led to never getting the education he needed to become the person he HAD to be to help so many. He could have partied in college instead of making crucial connections and he could have chased the money he was capable of making instead of what his heart was guiding him to do, missing out on the opportunity only he was prepared for to make a difference. Though there is no telling for certain, his decisions impacted his destiny and the destiny of thousands in his community.

Activity 2: _____

_____

_____

_____

_____

_____

_____

_____

_____

_____

_____

_____

_____

_____

_____

_____

_____

_____

_____

_____

_____

_____

_____

_____

_____

_____

_____

_____

_____

_____

_____

_____

_____

_____

If you are like most people who participate in this activity, you quickly realize that incredible things don't just happen to people overnight. A secret to success is that in all our doing, we can't just go through the motions; we have to become something. People define success in different ways; I personally am biased towards the definition given by a man with 10 NCAA Men's Basketball

National Championships, John Wooden. "Success is knowing that you did your best to become the best that you are capable of becoming." This can only come by being deliberate in our actions and intentions, not by going through the motions. You have to be something before you can accomplish truly great things.

Therefore, it's no question why *becoming* a life changing, impactful leader is the first step in *being* a life changing, impactful leader. There are no shortcuts for sustainable accomplishment, but once we understand the concept of becoming as more than an event, but as a process and even a lifestyle, there is no stopping what a man or woman can do to influence the world for good, starting with his or her own world and expanding from there as the revolution ascends ever upward.

Becoming a Leader

The truth is, far too many organizations operate under leadership teams who are sorely lacking in confidence, skill, and vision. Much of this can be attributed to that same myth that leadership is something you are born with, and therefore cannot be developed. We call this, the "either you have it or you don't" philosophy. Nothing could be further from the truth. In fact, a belief in such nonsense only leads to generations of organizational pitfalls. Leaders are developed every day. This book shows you exactly how that works and can continue to work over a lifetime, both of an individual and an organization.

For the sake of definition, here are three common assumptions and outcomes of those who believe in the "you either have it or you don't" philosophy.

Activity for Recognition: Put a check by or underline phrases that you have heard before OR outcomes you have seen:

☐ **Assumption 1:** A leader is a leader from the day he is born. You can ALWAYS tell who the leader is, even from youth.

☐ **Outcome:** The kid who is most outspoken or physically intimidating in school is given leadership positions from his or her youth. They grow up, operating under the same leadership principles they learned in grade school. Be charismatic, be charming, be intimidating, be vocal. The results are mixed but essentially almost all of an organization's finest resources in leadership are wasted when this attitude prevails because of the assumption that leaders are born and not made. Bottom lines are affected, morale is affected from the bottom up, and the destiny of the organization is affected, usually towards mediocrity because being the star football player in elementary school generally doesn't translate to efficient leadership practices in the workforce.

☐ **Assumption 2:** Leadership is solely dependent on one's experience. The more seasoned the organizational member, the better leader they will be.

☐ **Outcome:** Sometimes, and in the right situations, this is a decent thought. Most of the time it is not. Think about it, what if those experiences weren't very good experiences to begin with, filled with bad examples, poor decisions, and below average results? Then you are just perpetuating the "this is how it's always been" mentality, in which there is no room for innovation or growth, or frankly, success. There is an old saying that reads, "the amount of food you eat doesn't matter nearly as much as how you digest it." Your leadership experiences are only as good as the leader you become because of them.

☐ **Assumption 3**: Leadership is only a top of the organization practice. Everyone else is a "yes man" or a follower.

☐ **Outcome:** Failure! Harsh? Not really. Try it. See what happens (Don't really try it...). If there is one leader who is the sole source of knowledge and guidance for the organization, there is very little chance of long term survival once that leader retires or moves on. Furthermore, the brain power being tapped in regards to innovation, human resources, competency, and teamwork mentalities is a slight fraction of what it could be. This one pitfall is the functional equivalent to having a goal of driving two thousand miles on a quarter tank of gas. Best of luck!

Often as we travel the country and interact with leaders, we hear things like, "Well I learned to be a leader from my leader who learned it from his leader and that's just how things are done around here and I turned out OK." My response is always the same: "Turned out OK compared to what?" Sure, you turned out "OK" by your company's standards. Sadly, you'll never know what kind of leader you could have been, what kind of change you could have impacted with the right tools and the right organizational culture. It's the same in families. "My parents did 'this and that' and I turned out OK!" OK is not a convincing word and a family and a life are two very paramount things. You turned out OK, but compared to what? What could you have been?

Leaders are made, every day, molded by experience and guided in their development by important lessons and principles. It does not take much to be a bad leader, just get into a position of power, and then feel free to do what you want. Follow emotions over reason. Don't think about others and certainly don't think about consequences to your actions. Becoming a great leader, one who really inspires lasting change in the people and organizations around them, takes constant improvement, attention to the details of their own lives, and a willingness to learn and grow.

Improvement, becoming, constant progression. None of these mean perfection. Perfection was and never will be the goal. A closer parallel lies in learning and applying, every day. As Benjamin Franklin (whose quest for improvement will be explored in detail later in this book) once said, "Without continual growth and progress, such words as improvement, achievement, and success have no meaning." The power of becoming is the key and a gift offered to every human soul.

As we talked about before, you may think of a leader as someone beyond your skill set. Someone with a grand title or prestigious resume. This book will help you see that you ARE a leader. Once you know that you're a leader, this book will help you see the course to becoming the best leader, the leader who never stops improving and inspires others to take on the leadership mantle. When we wrote this book, zombie shows were popular. Think of it like a zombie apocalypse; your success as a zombie depends in large part on how many other people you can infect. The same principle is applied here. Your success as a leader depends in large part on your ability to elicit leadership from all those around you. Choose today to become a good leader and change people's' lives.

Become Vs. Becoming

At this point, you are beginning to understand what it means to become. Caterpillars become butterflies, accounting students become accountants, and people become leaders.

Here's the problem. To "become" is a one-time thing! A caterpillar becomes a butterfly exactly once. It's an important change, but it doesn't tell us the whole story. What kind of butterfly did you become? What personality? What flaws? How are you going to evolve beyond those flaws? Astounding leaders are in a constant state of **becoming,** while average leaders merely change their job title. This is the reason the leadership revolution has existed for generations. This is why it is timeless. We cannot just become when the evidence points to becoming. Don't settle. Resolve now to never stop becoming better. Resolve to take shake of the easy path and live a life of "becoming," and always look to build on what you have by seeking to become one thing and then another, etc. Becoming means there is no end destination, or if there was one, it was simply a springboard to something more.

The Chart on the following page illustrates the point.

BECOME	BECOMING
• A one-time destination.	• A lifestyle with unlimited upward milestones.
• Progresses to the point of comfort in their leadership style.	• Goes farther than their comfort zone, learning new skills and new strategies.
• May be a great leader, never losing their core values, but struggles to adapt.	• Has become a great leader but is already proactively adapting to the next generation of challenges without losing their core values.
• Expects their new organizational members to learn everything they can in their first year, just like they did.	• Expects to learn just as much as their new organization members, and is probably willing to learn from them.
• Is comfortable in their leadership level. • Knows they need to always grow but isn't too concerned about the how or when.	• Knows their leadership is effective, but is always looking to inspire one more team member, to be a little more effective, to go the extra mile for the good of the team. They feel you can always be better; you can always grow. Proactive.

If the Revolution is truly going to work in your life, your family, your team, or your organization, then it is imperative that the object of your desire is on becoming. No matter how fast or slow, it's always about becoming. If we settle for a one-time destination, we have missed the point. If we lift our view to the constant horizon before us, it is safe to say we will see and accomplish things well beyond the depths of our current desires.

WHAT MAKES A LEADER?

Successful leaders know it is not the quest for perfection in every aspect of their leadership that makes them effective, but in the courageous pursuit of the essentials and the necessary characteristics through which the greatest leadership moments are made. As a leader, you need to focus on your strengths while ensuring that weaknesses are brought to a level of neutrality, at the very least. That is a lot easier to handle than the thought of being everything at every moment of every day. Focus on becoming. The rest will fall into place.

Though there is no comprehensive list (and there never should be) on what makes up "the best" leaders; however, there are some indisputable characteristics both time and research have proven effective. We will give you ten to start with and invite you to add to the list as you progress in the leadership revolution. Remember, quality leadership and life changing initiatives are rarely by accident, and almost always will be the result of thought out, intelligent effort. Furthermore, remember that **who you are will always speak louder than what you do, and if you want lasting success, what you do should be a reflection of who you are.** Thus we will focus more on who you need to be than on tasks you need to do.

First, let's take a look at the list. These are the traits that have stuck out to us at the Allazo Group. Think of one of those successful leaders from before. Pick one who stands out to you for this activity. Put a checkmark next to the traits they exhibited.

Leadership Proficiencies

- Be Honest
- Be a Communicator
- Be Humble
- Be Inspiring
- Be a Visionary
- Be Consistent
- Be an Expert
- Be Decisive
- Be Resourceful
- Be Accountable

How did your leader hold up? If you are like most people who participate in this exercise, your leader was probably honest. It's almost nearly impossible to be an effective leader when there is an aura of dishonesty that surrounds you. BUT, after number one, if you are like most people, your leader is probably all over the place in their check marks.

What does this tell us? One can be an effective leader, not through perfection, but by being true to their strengths. That is great news for every aspiring leader on the planet! Go back through and put a check on the other side of the traits that you think you are naturally gifted with. Was that an encouraging experience? It should be, because these are some of the things you can start focusing on today.

Now, one final point before we explore the traits more in depth. Not being exceptional at a trait is not the same as being horrible at a trait. A neutral rating will not bring you down as a leader if there are other things you excel at. Most great leaders AT LEAST break neutral in one of the ten characteristics we have highlighted. Go ahead and run through the list one more time, putting a negative mark next to the traits in which your leader is absolutely horrible, to the point where it affected their capability to be a leader. Chances are there was no more than one negative trait, if there were any at all. Now try the same thing with the WORST leader you've ever had (no really, take a second and try it). See the difference? It is night and day when we know what we are looking for, and the path of becoming is a lot clearer under the light of these experiences.

Let's explore each of the traits in a little more detail. Feel encouraged to take notes of your thoughts as we go:

1 – Be Honest

"The high road is always respected. Honesty and integrity are always rewarded."

- Scott Hamilton, Figure Skating World Champion

A working definition of being honest is being truthful in both what we say to others and what we say to ourselves. Integrity, which falls under honesty, is doing the right thing, for the right reasons whether or not anyone is watching. We are only truly honest when we possess both.

Honesty is more than just not telling lies to those you work with, it is having integrity in both word and deed. There is nothing which will more quickly destroy a leader than a lack of honesty. History teaches you that. Your experiences teach you that. However, true honesty is a powerful tool in endearing you to those you lead. Let us show you a powerful example.

We are lucky enough to associate with a man, whose company he personally grew from a tiny start up, eventually ended selling it in the range of a billion dollars. One day, he realized that he forgot to pick up a ream of paper from the store earlier that day as his wife requested him to. So what did he do? He went into the back room of his large office on a large corporate campus, consisting of multiple three story buildings owned by him, and grabbed a ream of paper. Before he left for the day, he made sure the secretary in the Human Resources department deducted the full price of that ream of paper from his paycheck. His integrity was of far higher importance than the five or so dollars the ream of paper would have cost his billion-dollar company.

On a scale from 1-10, considering every aspect of your life from home to work, how honest have you been in the last month?

Answer: _____

What needs to change right now, to make you a more honest and ethical leader?

Answer: _____

_____
_____
_____
_____
_____
_____

2 – Be a Communicator

*"Communication- the human connection- is
the key to personal and career success."*

- Paul J. Meyer, International Best Selling Author

When people think of communication, they often think of public speaking. An informal survey was conducted on the topic of people's biggest fears. Death came in second while public speaking came in first. Thus by this same logic, most people in the world fear giving the eulogy as opposed to the alternative. Luckily, public speaking is only one way a leader might be an effective communicator, and it should be a relief that it certainly isn't a prerequisite.

The power to communicate does not lie solely in the ability to express passionately in front of a large crowd. It is a skill developed in the everyday conversations with team members, electronically, in person, and even in one's body language. If you want to be a more effective communicator, it may not be as hard as you think. The key is to build trust. Authentic trust! Here are a few suggestions:

-   **Be Personable.** Start with simple things, like sharing your personal experiences in the organization. When possible, do this on a one-on-one level, not in a large group setting. Encourage your team members to do the same, sharing both their positive and negative experiences with you as you reinforce the positive actions they contribute on a daily basis. Be sure to take notes after each conversation. Make the extra effort to remember the details.

Take an interest in people's personal lives. Recognize and acknowledge that there's more to life than the organization and express belief in their talents and abilities. People don't care how much you know until they know how much you care, so care! Help your team members develop trust in your leadership through the trust they have in your authentic care for them. This doesn't just apply to senior level leaders, but to leaders with no title at all.

What can you do today to better help people see your gratitude for their unique talents and abilities?

_____

_____

_____

_____

_____

_____

_____

_____

_____

How many times a day are you complimenting people (go ahead and count on an average day, pushing yourself to act completely normal)? _____

How many times would you like to communicate this way on any given day? _____

- **Be on the team, not against the team.** Picture This: A quarterback is a starter for his squad but distant from his team, worries about his own statistics, and is constantly belittling his teammates in front of his coaches and management. How well would that go over if you were one of his teammates?

Now Picture This: Derek Jeter, known by his nickname "the Captain", was easily one of the greatest New York Yankees to ever live. His name exists in an exclusive circle that includes such men as Babe Ruth, Joe DiMaggio, and Lou Gehrig. He may also be one of the best examples of a leader in being on the team and not against the team. One of his defining characteristics was that he was always willing to sacrifice himself for the team and was never accused of sacrificing the team for himself. That can't be said for far too many leaders.

Jeter led without fanfare during his twenty year career in the Bronx. It was said by his teammates that at practice, he was always the first person on the field to take ground balls and the last person off the field. That was a message to his teammates more powerful than any speech he could have given.

- **Stay on the message.** Once your organization sees the desired destination, and we will discuss that later on, it is your job as a leader to point out again and again, where you are going and why you are going there. Ideally, it comes up in every meeting, every planning session, or every conversation.

You cannot afford to have a New Year's resolution mentality, where goals are preached strongly for a week and then steadily drift away to make room for new, unfocused trends or objectives. One of the most powerful characteristics of effective communicators is the ability to consistently stay on the message which is most important to their organization. They are masters at avoiding the distractions and short sighted messages that could easily disrupt the way to lasting success.

What is one main message you wish to convey in every communication opportunity? Why?

_____

_____

_____

_____

_____

_____

_____

_____

- **Keep Your Door Open.** Personal communication is only effective if you are available for communication! As a leader, take time to keep your door open. Be available to your team. Build trust through making your office a place of learning.

If the only time people enter your office, or into your presence, is to receive a reprimand, it will make communication that builds people difficult, if not impossible. If you're office is a place of positivity and growth, you will be able to have difficult conversations with confidence that trust has already been established. You will have invested the time and emotion into building those around you, opening the lines of authentic communication in the process, while resisting the temptation to lead by suppressing thought and implementing scare tactics.

3 – Be Humble

"Humility is not thinking less of yourself, it's thinking of yourself less."

- C. S. Lewis

A true leader knows that his or her most valuable resource lies not only in their knowledge, but in the collective knowledge of all they interact with. Synonyms of being humble include words such as modesty, lack of pride, and, submissiveness. It is coming to an honest opinion that is not proliferated by one's opinion of themselves or their position. Many find it harder said than done.

Being humble is believing that though you may be the leader of the organization, team, department, or group, you are not the organization, team, department, or group. The humble leader realizes the organization is made up of individuals with different experiences and talent sets than them. Thus, they know there is more than one leader, and they believe it's the way it should be. Both their speech and their actions reflect it. As one successful American basketball coach stated, "Humility is the true key to success. Successful people lose their way at times. They often embrace and overindulge from the fruits of success. Humility halts this arrogance and self-indulging trap. Humble people share the credit and wealth, remaining focused and hungry to continue the journey of success."

A humble leader trusts easily, forgives easily, and walks the way they preach. They are not pushovers in any sense of the word. Pushover and humility are not synonyms. Rather, humble leaders are focused on the vision and are readily willing to admit when something or someone isn't working or living up to their potential. They also admit their own mistakes and take the time to invest in individuals. In the words of Pennsylvania founder, William Penn, "Sense shines with a double luster when it is set in humility. An able and yet humble man is a jewel worth a kingdom." Or possibly a jewel to those who follow them.

4 – Be Inspiring

"Our chief want is someone who will inspire
us to be what we know we could be."

- Ralph Waldo Emerson

Being inspiring can mean giving motivational speeches, but more often than not, the truly inspiring leader is the one who does the little things, day in and day out, to inspire their team members to reach a little higher and believe in themselves a little more. That inspiration is the catalyst for the drive towards uncommon results.

To increase your inspirational capabilities, look to do a couple things every day:

- Share stories that illustrate organizational ideals. This can happen in a one-on-one situation, a small group setting, and companywide whenever possible.
- Show others who they can become. Too many people go through life feeling they are constantly hitting a wall. Often all that is needed is for someone to believe in them. It is amazing how people rise to the level of their leader's positive reinforcement.
- When given the choice to lift someone up or tear someone down, choose to lift them up.
- Be as passionate as anyone else in your organization about what you do and why you do it.
- Be a realist, but with an optimistic attitude.
- In all things, lead by example and help people see the good in themselves while simultaneously preaching results that must come based on a team member's capabilities. If you do, it is hard to go wrong.

5 – Be a Visionary

"You are not here merely to make a living.
You are here in order to enable the world to live
more amply, with greater vision, with a finer
spirit of hope and achievement. You are here to
enrich the world, and you impoverish yourself if
you forget the errand."

- American President Woodrow Wilson

A visionary leader is one who has put his or her house in order. It is impossible to guide your team across a vast ocean into uncharted territories when all your attention is spent plugging up leaks in your boat.

Visionary leaders need substance. Often when visionary leadership is brought up, what is actually heard by team members is something like this, "Alright guys, we're not doing so well right now, but this month we're going to do better. So go out and get it done!" There is no substance in these kinds of statements and their negative effects far outweigh the positive.

Visionary leaders not only have substance in their statements, but plans with their predictions. A truly visionary leader is open to all types of information, and is quick to turn that information into a strategy which leads to the team's ultimate goal. Visionary leaders encourage innovation, see obstacles and opportunities before others do, and above all else, are committed and persistent in their creativity. A visionary leader is not tied to the traditional ways of doing things, but only to the vision of what their team can become. Couple belief with a road map, and you will become a powerful resource to those around you.

6 – Be Consistent

"The secret of success is consistency of purpose."

- Former British Prime Minister, Benjamin Disraeli

Be consistently consistent in what consistently works. This can only be done if you establish a cause to be consistent about! Otherwise the alternatives are being consistent in error or consistent in inconsistency. Neither one of those are good options! You've seen this kind of inconsistency, we've seen this kind of inconsistency, and chances are you are thinking of a few examples right now.

Consistency at its best involves regular routines grounded in good habits. It means converting to a message and keeping that message alive in everything you decide, think, or do. At it's best, consistency involves being consistent in the way you treat others above you, below you, and around you. It is being the same person on Monday that you are on Friday, and bing the same person with your team members as you are with your CEO who may just be visiting for a day.

What kind of consistent actions do those around you need to see to reach their full potential?

_____
_____
_____
_____
_____

What are some habits that need to become a consistent part of your life in order to help you be the person and leader you want to be?

_____

_____

_____

_____

_____

_____

_____

We had the opportunity of working with an organization who struggled to trust their management. When we investigated the cause, it was really quite simple. When the CEO of the company came around for monthly visits, management worked hard to sweep all issues under the rug, encourage employees to change day-to-day routines, and above all else, to put on a smiling face for a day trying to give off the impression that those traits were rooted deep within that branch of the organization. Employees were using words such as facade, lies, and "putting on a show." This lack of consistency directly resulted in a lack of trust. A lack of trust directly resulted in a lack of production. Furthermore, it is no wonder that within two years the turnover within that branch was above 90 percent!

Consistency in your actions breeds consistency in others. If you have a purpose, and your decisions and conversations perfectly reflect that purpose, you will increase the likelihood of others buying in and reflecting that same "why" behind what they do. This is the essence of true, persuasive leadership.

7 – Be an Expert

"An investment in knowledge pays the best interest."

- Benjamin Franklin

You don't need to know everything, but you need to be ever learning. Learning is the catalyst for application, and it is only in application that change can occur. An expert in any field will not know all the answers, but they will know more than most, and their real genius will be in finding answers that others cannot.

There are a number of things "experts" realize that others do not. Which of these are you applying? Which of these can you implement? An expert:

- **Stays up on new technology and innovation**. This is mostly driven by excitement, the kind of excitement that can only come from a rooted passion in their field. The best experts we know collect things such as engineering magazines, teacher websites, and technology blogs the same way kids today collect video games and text messages. At dinner parties, they are just as excited, if not more excited, to talk about their industry as they are about any current event. In a conversation one of us had with one of the United States highest ranking judges in Washington DC, he indicated that even though he has reached the peak of his career, he is still a political junkie, spending his free time listening to talk radio, and reading up on the latest political news and ideas. If there is brewing innovation, he wants to know about it and that is one of the biggest reasons to which he credits his success. As you follow your passions, success seems to follow.

- **Learns from those around them**. There is something you can learn from anyone, good or bad. Let's focus on the good people have to offer. The key is being teachable. Chances are, everyone in your organization knows at least one thing in your field that you don't know. If you go into conversations looking to add to your sphere of knowledge, you will notice an excitement that can only come from being in the habit of inquiring. If you are diligent enough to write down the things you learn and review them at the end of the day, you will find yourself an expert in the eyes of others rather quickly. If you take the time to thank those who teach you, no matter their position, you will find that they will be just as excited to share more as you are to receive more.

- **Solves Problems**. We conduct a lot of interviews with a lot of people. One theme which has emerged under solving problems and being an expert is that people who are willing to face problems in their organization head on, generally are seen as experts by those around them. This is not without reason. Those who take the time and extra effort to be problem solvers, and not merely problem reporters, have access to a special kind of learning that accelerates experience and broadens understanding.

- **Reads**. Theodore Roosevelt is widely regarded as one of the most intelligent presidents in the history of the United States. He is also remembered for being an avid, even ferocious reader, devouring at least one book a day (365 books a year, about 2,737 books over the course of his presidency). That is an amazing feat. What we recommend to harness that same intellect which is available to all of us, is taking a topic in which you wish to become an expert and finding the top seven respected works on that subject. Read at least one of those works every two weeks, underlining, highlighting, and making notes as you go until you've completed your list. There is no reason to miss out on what others have discovered before you, and there is no substitute for deep and informative reading.

What is ONE specific subject you wish to master in your specific field? Talk to people in your organization, browse book lists and respected blogs, and then come up with your own top seven list below.

Book 1:
Book 2:
Book 3:
Book 4:
Book 5:
Book 6:
Book 7:

8 – Be Decisive

"It's not hard to make decisions when you know what your values are."

- Roy Disney, Brother to Walt Disney and Cofounder of The Disney Corporation

The decisiveness of leaders is key to organizational progression and the avoidance of organizational paralysis by analysis. Decisions should be well thought out, of course, but it is not often that an idea alone can really change the world. There has to be concentrated action. Nothing beats beginning like beginning, and it is the leader's job to lead the way in beginnings or to support them both vocally and in action.

Being well informed is a precursor to confidence in one's decisions. There will still be times where course corrections are needed or when unforeseen events will take precedence; but being well informed will serve you far more efficiently than a habit of shooting from the hip.

Two examples: The first is with a school we worked with. A teacher asked her administrator for permission to do a fun, low-risk activity with her kids. Normally, this would be a simple yes and it started with a tentative yes and permission to let the kids know of their special activity, a pajama party, where they would read books all day and have a Dr. Seuss movie. However, the senior leader of the school had tensions with his own leaders in the administration office. This ultimately forced him into a state of indecisiveness. That indecisiveness caused months to go by and no answer to be given, even with the teacher respectfully asking week after week. Eventually, this lack of trust in the decision making of others affected the student's attitudes and motivations, as it's the students in a school who are usually the quickest to pick up on conflict and uncertainty around them.

The second example is of a senior leader in a large organization. He knew his objectives, he knew his purpose, and he knew the values of his organization, inside and out. This caused him to trust his leader's decisions, and in turn, his leaders trusted his judgement. He developed a habit of being well informed by the right people and being decisive. The story goes like this, given to us by one of his colleagues. When this leader would start with the decision that needed to be made, he would contemplate the issue, then gather everyone who had a stake in the issue into his office, and would go through all the questions he had. If one of his team members didn't know the answer to his question, he would simply ask, "Who would know the answer?" If that person was in the office, he would pull them in to answer the question. If that person was out of the office, he would get them in on a conference call. Apparently, this often led to up to ten people on a conference call, an overcrowded office, and some extremely late nights. But once all the information was on the table, more often than not, the decision was obvious. The senior leader would then without reservation make the decision, delegate responsibility, and have everyone report back to him in the morning. Not only did his employees trust his decisiveness, they also trusted his process and in turn, achieved an uncommon state of unity.

9 – Be Resourceful

"While no one is expected to leap tall buildings in a single bound, our aspiring heroes will be tested on their courage, integrity, self-sacrifice, compassion, and resourcefulness - the stuff of all true superheroes"

- Stan Lee, Founder of Marvel Comics

Time and time again, the concept of many brains led by a resourceful leader are far more powerful than one brain who refuses the help of others. Most successes in organizations are a team effort. Embrace it, and you are embracing success.

In the twenty first century, the greatest resource at a leader's disposal is human intelligence. The knowledge of an informed and educated team will almost always be greater than the knowledge of any single individual. Therefore, a leader's job is to help others use their talents and skills to benefit the greater good of the team.

Nurture those talents in others and help others to see the talents within them. Believe that leadership is a team process and don't put off letting others onto the team! Establish a clear and defined culture of sharing: sharing knowledge, sharing resources, or sharing goals. Don't spend too much time looking for the next big thing when the next big thing might very well be sitting in the notebook or brewing thoughts of someone right within your organization. Above all, understand what's around you and put it to work every day for the benefit of your team.

Time and time again the concept of many brains led by a resourceful leader are far more powerful than one brain who refuses the help of others. Most successes in organizations are a team effort. Embrace it and you are embracing success.

10 – Be Accountable

"It is not only what we do, but also what we
do not do, for which we are accountable."

- Jean-Baptiste Poquelin, 17th Century French Playwright and Actor

To expect accountability out of others, you must first be accountable to yourself. Are you walking the walk or are you merely talking the talk? The contrast, as described in this old saying, really does make all the difference. Hypocritical actions and rhetoric wash away credibility like the evening tide rolling over abandoned sand castles.

As a leader, do not kid yourself with the idea that what you do does not matter. On the contrary, it is not just what you do that greatly affects others, but also what you say, what you believe, and what you demonstrate in your attitude. It is also what you *don't* do. Take the example of Benjamin Franklin as a guide as he was a master in self accountability. For much of his life, Franklin would pick a particular attribute he wished to develop and would keep a scorecard on which every night, he would give himself a score for his adherence to that virtue for that particular day. Once he felt like he mastered that virtue, he would move on to a new virtue.

To increase performance, you should seek to be accountable to someone. However, you can also apply a version of Benjamin Franklin's self-accountability method into your own life.

For example, you may keep a tally of your conversations with your family members over the course of the day. You may find that, to your surprise, when you are really accountable to yourself, you see that eighty percent of your conversations contain at least one unnecessary negative comment. This would be the perfect opportunity to apply the modified self-accountability method. We will walk you through it.

Start with a clearly defined result you wish to obtain. At present, 80 percent of my conversations with family members contain a negative comment that distracts from my message of love and brings a feeling of negativity to those around me. I will reverse this to where 80 percent of my conversations will not contain unnecessary negative comments (after you reach 80 percent, it will be much easier to set and obtain a goal of 100 percent over the course of a day, week, month, and then year!).

Keep a scorecard. After each conversation you have with a family member, take a moment to reflect and then mark down a tally in either a "No Negative Comment" Section or a "Negative Comment Section". If something really jumps out at you during the conversation, you can also write down that inspiration underneath your tally marks. It can be as simple as something like this:

No Negative Comment	Negative Comment
IIII - If I take the time to think about what I am going to say before I say it, removing negative comments is much easier.	I

Review. At the end of each day, review the progress of your desired outcome. For example, what went well in your decision to have positive conversations? What made the difference (was it your environment, state of mind, new perspective)? What didn't go well? What can you change for tomorrow? This can easily be answered in a couple of sentences on the back of your score card.

Record. Keep all of your score cards to review them and look for trends. This will help you to have clearer objectives going forward. At the end of every day, record your percentage on a calendar or a chart so you can see your progress. When you hit your target one week in a row, you are ready to add another objective, but you can always go back to your previous objectives any time you feel the need! This is a marathon of self-mastery, not a sprint.

So now it's your turn... Think of one item in which you can begin to be accountable to yourself starting today. Fill out the details below to maximize your progress!

Clear Objective:

Keep a Scorecard:

Review: What Questions are you going to ask yourself EVERY day?

_____

_____

_____

_____

_____

_____

_____

_____

_____

_____

Record: If you don't have a system that works for you, you can use this simple 30-day chart!

Day 1:

Day 2:

Day 3:

Day 4:

Day 5:

Day 6:

Day 7:

Day 8:

Day 9:

Day 10:

Day 11:

Day 12:

Day 13:

Day 14:

Day 15:

Day 16:

Day 17:

Day 18:

Day 19:

Day 20:

Day 21:

Day 22:

Day 23:

Day 24:

Day 25:

Day 26:

Day 27:

Day 28:

Day 29:

Day 30:

Reflection

When you think of these 10 traits that great leaders are proven to possess (or as we said, mostly possess), what else comes to mind that you would add to the list? Why do you feel these additional traits are important, especially in your current leadership role? As you go along in the book, we would invite you to add at least three more traits of life changing leaders that you have personally observed.

_____

_____

_____

_____

_____

_____

_____

_____

_____

_____

_____

_____

_____

_____

_____

_____

_____

_____

_____

_____

_____

Remember, the initial internalization of these principles and making them a part of who you are is only one step on the spiral staircase of the leadership revolution. For example, once you feel you are good at being decisive, strive to focus on becoming great at being decisive, and then exceptional, and then extraordinary, and on and on over the course of a lifetime until you become a master of decisiveness. Since you will always be a leader, you will always have room to improve towards mastery that inspires, encourages, and benefits those around you.

What Real Leaders Should NEVER Do

Just as there are indisputable qualities that make up the highly effective leader, there are, sadly, traits and habits that define the world's worst leaders, leaders found in non-profits, sports teams and student councils just as much as businesses. In fact, we would go as far as to say that these traits disqualify a person from maintaining the title of a true leader. We want to make you aware of five of these traits. There are many more, of course, but we feel these five are crucial. You are invited to add to this list and to review it often, not to get yourself down, but to remind yourself of the challenge we are giving you in this moment to always strive to be the opposite.

The Traits and Habits that Stifle Leadership

Real Leaders Never:

- Lie
- Talk Down to People
- Ignore The Power of Example
- Decline to Take Responsibility
- Take Credit for the Work of Others

Let's take a look and examine these for a moment. Do you see any of this in you, around you, or on the horizon within your organization?

1. **Real Leaders Never Lie**. The sad reality is that telling a lie is often much easier than telling the truth, especially when the pressure is on and you feel like your reputation is at stake. But how often does that really work out? We would say that it never works out because there are only two scenarios that come from a pattern of lying. First, your lie eventually catches up to you. Or two, you get away with the lie and find it easier and easier to lie again. As opposed to the ascension associated with the leadership revolution, this is the spiral staircase downward into destructive habits that will ruin all credibility you may have built up over the course of your career. Even if your bosses don't catch on to you, those around you will, and as a result, all trust will be lost. Best bet? If it all starts with one lie, don't choose to lie.

2. **Real Leaders Never Talk Down to People**. This is a generic habit that encompasses a lot of common things found in organizations. Really, it all starts with attitude, usually some sort of inferiority complex or a level of entitlement and self-aggrandizing. The way you choose to talk to people is a direct reflection of how much respect you deserve and has little to do with the day-to-day actions of your subordinates or equals. It's not just about the Golden Rule; it's about the fact that if you REALLY feel the need to patronize, you probably aren't doing your job right. If you choose to use words, tones, or a speed of communication that clearly send a message of inferiority, you should expect a lack of respect and a lack of growth that will benefit your team. If you are looking to stay the "Top Dog" and take more pride in your position as a manager, (because you certainly aren't a leader), then it's time to take a good long look in the mirror and reprioritize your career. In the words of JK Rowling, "If you want to know what a man's like, take a good look at how he treats his inferiors, not his equals."

How do you treat those "below you" on the organizational chart as opposed to those who have a direct effect on your next promotion or pay raise?

_____

_____

_____

_____

_____

_____

_____

_____

_____

3. **Real leaders never ignore the power of example**. "Do as I say, not as I do" is a recipe for disaster. What you do speaks far louder than what you say. It is a theme repeated time and time again in all the teachings of The Allazo Group, but especially in this book. The most powerful way to lead is by example. To ignore your example's influence is to eliminate accountability to yourself for your actions. A lot of money is spent on hiring consultants like us to figure out dysfunctionality, when it takes about five minutes for an outsider to figure out the dysfunctionality starts with an out-of-touch leader, or more likely, a leader in denial. Words are useless without action. This idea has been around for centuries. In fact, Shakespeare in his play *Richard III*, written in 1594, includes a character known in history only as "the First Murderer". His statement is clear,

"Fear not, my lord, we will not stand to prate;

Talkers are no good doers: be assured

We come to use our hands and not our tongues."

A good "doer" always has more lasting influence than a good "sayer". A good "doer" who is also a good "sayer" is a powerful combination in leadership.

4. **Real leaders never decline to take responsibility.** No one likes to fail. No one likes to look bad. No one likes that feeling of dread when it comes down to admitting fault. But when things go wrong, there are no excuses. If you choose to be a leader, you choose to take responsibility for failures just as much as you may be

privileged to be praised for successes. As a leader, you always have a "Get Out of Jail Free Card" that can be played at any time. In essence, it is just putting the blame on someone else, or throwing them under a metaphorical bus. But every time this is done, a leader's capacity for good decreases just like the battery of a cell phone. Once the battery is dead, the phone is essentially useless.

On the flip side, the leader who chooses to own up to the failures of themselves and their team are the leaders who should be held in the highest regard. Why? It shows not only are you a team player, but that you understand your role on the team. It shows you have integrity, confidence, and an understanding of your responsibility. In turn, those around you know that if they do not demonstrate the same traits, there is simply no excuse.

5. **Real Leaders Never Take Credit for the Work of Others**. In her Forbes article from April 2013, Jacquelyn Smith dives into this problem of leaders taking credit for other people's work with both profound insight and excellent research. The full article can be found on the Forbes website, but let's take a look at the part of it that most pertains to why this leadership fail takes place. She writes:

"Power grabs can happen in any corporate environment because the system is simply set up for competition," says Lynn Taylor, workplace expert and author of *Tame Your Terrible Office Tyrant*. "However, there is healthy and unhealthy competition. This variety breeds backstabbing and a pandemic of the glory hog syndrome. The uncertain economy and still relatively high unemployment also creates fertile ground for job insecurity and credit stealing. So the practice becomes a misguided insurance against being on the chopping block."

Taylor says bosses may think, *I have to be accountable for all the bad news and mistakes, why not take credit for all the good?* "Unfortunately, those moments of glory and style of management will be fleeting. It will soon erode the dedication and results of the hard working staff behind all the kudos."

Teri Hockett, the chief executive of What's For Work?, a career site for women, says some workplaces instill a strong commitment to teamwork and employee recognition to prevent this type of situation. "This allows the very best ideas and people in the organization to rise," she says. "On the other hand, it's not uncommon for bosses to take credit for the work of their employees, for many different reasons."

Reason one: some bosses believe that they are entitled to own everything their team produces, Hockett says. "And since many deal with plenty of challenges, from poor earnings to upset customers and delayed projects, at some point they'll want to showcase something positive as their own, even if their employee produced the work."

Reason two: many companies allow this type of behavior by not having clear guidelines and value statements in place that stress the importance of recognizing employees for their work, Hockett adds.

"Then there are bosses who feel threatened by certain employees," Hockett explains. "Maybe the employee is smarter or produces ideas that others find valuable." If a boss feels threatened, they might take credit for their employee's work to prevent exposing their own shortcomings.

Finally, she says, a boss might take credit because of the competitive job market and high unemployment rate. "Some bosses believe they must protect their role at all costs, so the idea of elevating their employee's work contribution makes them uncomfortable."

The problem is that "at all costs" consists of a lot of things that are unethical, irresponsible, and would just be seen as wrong in every setting outside of work. The whole concept of "it's just business" is rarely used outside of the context of justifying something you would never think to do in any other setting because of its absurdity of principle.

To Sum It Up: It takes a big person to be a leader. Not big in stature or in speech, but big in the ways that count: confidence, integrity, teamwork, and shared successes. They may be big steps in the becoming stage of the Leadership Revolution, but they are essential for developing the strength to courageously climb onward and upward.

We Become What We Constantly Practice and Surround Ourselves With

There is no secret that we become what we constantly associate with. This doesn't just have to do with the people we spend time with, but also with the thoughts we choose to think, the media we choose to view, the conversations we choose to have, and ultimately, the life we choose to live. At the end of the day, these are all choices that belong to us, and these same choices not only define us, but mold our character into the positive or to the negative.

To have high character, we have to have high standards. One foot firmly in the realm of rationalization and one in the realm of excellence is really taking no stance at all, except for the stance that you are not willing to commit to excellence in your personal or professional life. It is best to have both feet firmly set on solid ground. This way, it is much harder to slip.

In one of the previous sections, we talked about ten of the characteristics that define true leadership, we have also talked about the flaws that destroy leadership. These characteristics don't just manifest themselves in external actions, but often in thought and desire. In fact, that makes sense, right? Nobody just wakes up one day and decides to steal a million dollars. The thought has to cross their mind first, and then somehow that thought has to turn into a desire strong enough for a plan. Only then is the action actually manifested.

So, to look at it the other way, if we choose not to ignore those inner desires to be the kind of leader we always thought we would be, that desire can carry us a long way. The desire leads to deep thought and reflection, even to learning of the characteristics of great leaders. Those thoughts turn into plans, both in mind or written out (preferably), which ultimately lead to action.

In the following section, we will talk about surrounding ourselves with the right people. In this section, the focus is on surrounding ourselves with the right thoughts and actions, as well as the right physical environment. Data has proven that our attitudes not only affect our quality of life, but can affect the happiness and satisfaction of those around us, especially in the workplace. What we choose to surround ourselves with affects our attitude, outlook on life, and everyday situations. Let's make a list of things we have complete control over when choosing what we will become. These are things that we absorb into our lives, one way or another, and they have a direct effect on our becoming. Some may be more important than others, but they all send a message both to the outside world and the world of our own mind.

1. The shows we watch
2. The books we read
3. The words we use
4. The cleanliness, or lack thereof, of our personal space
5. The thoughts we choose to think
6. The food we choose to eat
7. The clothes we choose to wear
8. The attitude we choose to have
9. _____
10. _____
11. _____
12. _____

What else would you add to this list? Fill in the blanks. Surround yourself with good things and you can expect to become better. It's simple logic. If you eat horribly and never jog, you will not become a marathon runner. If you eat like a marathon runner and train like a marathon runner, you won't have a problem running a marathon. Or in another analogy, if you choose to wrestle with the pigs, you should expect to get muddy.

What kind of message do your actions and surroundings send to both your conscience and those around you?

_____

_____

_____

_____

_____

_____

_____

_____

Working with Mentors

A mentor is a powerful, and we would even say, indisputable strength and resource for any leader at any level of the Leadership Revolution. A mentor is a trusted adviser, within your organization or outside of it, who is willing to be turned to for council, insights, and guidance. This is a valuable advantage as you progress along your path as a leader. Though mentors are usually associated with those starting their career, we have seen there is a great case to be made that even senior leaders can benefit from a close mentor relationship. Under the premise there is always someone who knows a little more, has a little more experience, or someone who you can talk things out with, every leader can use a mentor.

There are also several practical benefits to having a mentor. One would be that you have someone you can turn to whose real desire is to help you succeed. They have already found their career's success and people who have found success often find joy in helping others succeed as well. Another reason, as stated earlier, is simply that you become who you choose to associate with, so why not choose to associate with someone who inspires you to become better? No matter who we interact with, we are constantly hearing and seeing messages, intended and unintended. When you recognize something you don't want to be, it is your responsibility to block that message out. When you see something you want to be, it is your responsibility to surround yourself with that message and work to make it a part of who you are.

Think of the five people you spend the most time with and write them down here:

1.
2.
3.
4.
5.

If you are the sum total of all the characteristics (both good and bad) of these five people, what kind of person are you?

_____

_____

_____

_____

_____

_____

_____

_____

_____

With that said, what do you need to change to BECOME the leader you desire to be?

_____

_____

_____

_____

_____

_____

_____

_____

Often times, mentors will naturally find you as a result of the law of attraction. If you are seeking to be taught, a teacher will often come out of seemingly nowhere. This isn't as much a phenomenon as it is that the teacher was there all along, you just finally started looking.

Whatever the circumstances may be, there are certain things you want in a mentor. The first and most obvious thing is that it needs to be someone you actually want to emulate. This isn't as much about a specific career title as much as it is about if they've applied the principles of success you wish to adopt. This also includes a deep devotion to ethics and leading with integrity. A mentor who leads you down a road not lined with integrity is no mentor at all. Finally, a mentor must be willing to give freely without any political gain. A mentor, by definition, is someone who has knowledge and is willing to give it without thought of using that relationship to climb any sort of ladder in the process. A true mentor respects that confidentiality, gives freely, and expects you to act on the advice given to you.

Once you've identified and established a formal or informal relationship with your mentor, there are several assumed rules it's best that you follow.

Rule 1 - Listen and Observe. You will make the most of your experience if you commit to being a true listener. Take notes and write down reflections after each meeting with your mentor. In addition to what your mentor says, observe how they conduct themselves, how you perceive they made life decisions, and pay close attention to their pattern of thinking. The goal is not just to learn to do the things they do, but to think the way they think.

Rule 2 - Come with Specific Questions. Don't expect your mentor to do all the work. Although, conversations will likely flow naturally, your mentor can't read your mind. Have specific questions in mind and make sure those questions pertain to your mentor. For example, you can ask anybody "How do you make good career choices?" It's a decent question but with someone specific in front of you, it might be more helpful to ask something like, "Mr. Smith, given your thirty years of experience in leadership positions in various industries, what would you say are the most important things to consider when making career decisions?" You will gain more out of asking specific questions you have prepared beforehand than general questions when you are struggling to find something to ask.

Rule 3 - Show Gratitude. Your mentor's time is valuable. Treat it with the utmost respect. If you make an appointment, keep it. Make sure to always say thank you and even write a thank you card when appropriate. Let your mentor know that you understand the sacrifice they are making to invest in you, and that what they share does not go unobserved. Make sure to follow up and let them know what you did with their advice the next time you have the opportunity to meet with them. As said by the late and great Zig Ziglar, "Gratitude is the healthiest of all human emotions. The more you express gratitude for what you have,the more likely you will have even more to express gratitude for."

Rule 4 - Maintain Confidences. It is likely that some of the information and advice your mentor shares with you will be meant for your ears only. It is critical that you take this seriously and always maintain the highest level of confidentiality. Nothing will halt your mentor relationship quicker than taking a private conversation and making it public. If your mentor wanted that information public, they would probably write a blog. You don't need to write it for them. The more your mentor can trust your integrity the more they are likely to invest in you in the way of time and knowledge.

Rule 5 - Come with Ideas, Not Just Problems. A mentor is not a problem solver but more of an adviser. Their job is to teach you principles and it is your job is to apply them. You won't get much in way of becoming an exceptional leader and progressing through the leadership revolution if all you have is a set of problems. Instead, think deeply of the challenges and opportunities presented to you and write down some creative solutions and why you think they might work. Share these with your mentors and allow them to coach you and further help you to develop your own ideas. Remember, as said before, your goal should not be to simply learn what to do, but why to do it. Your mission is to learn how to think like a leader!

What if You're the Mentor?

Conversely, as you become a more powerful and effective leader, the Leadership Revolution will often put you in a position to be a mentor. This is a wonderful opportunity to learn and give. It is also an excellent chance to invest in the health of your organization. Just like that of a protégé, there are several rules you should follow.

Rule 1 - Don't Make It About You. It is easy for a mentor to feel a boost of pride and even confidence when given the opportunity to guide another person. Whatever you do, do not let it go to your head! Some may think bragging about your accomplishments is mentoring, but really, it's just promoting a self-centered attitude that protégés could easily emulate, leading to destructive behavior down the road. You are proving nothing and giving nothing unless you let the protégé take the lead and use you as a guide in their very personal and very specific journey through the leadership revolution.

Rule 2 - Establish Boundaries. Mentoring relationships can become inappropriate if clear boundaries are not set. This does not call for over formality or a cold demeanor, rather a clear understanding of expectations from both parties. You should expect the person you are mentoring to follow up with you, to come to meetings prepared and to not expect you to solve their problems. Conversely, they should expect you to honor your commitments, give clear and honest guidance, and be a support to them as they ascend in the revolution towards leadership excellence.

Rule 3 - Show Integrity. Your word is your bond. If you accept the opportunity to be a mentor, you accept the responsibility to set the example of the highest level of integrity, no matter what position you may hold. It is the essential duty of a mentor to lead the way in building a generation of ethical leadership. If you have made mistakes in the past, own up to them, learn from them, and don't allow them to be repeated by those who look to you for guidance. Expect complete, absolute integrity from yourself and the same level of integrity from those you mentor.

Rule 4 - Maintain Confidences. As you strive to make your mentoring relationship not only effective but a safe environment for growth, you will have many things shared with you. This is a compliment to the good work you are doing. It is a sign of mutual respect and admiration. You don't want to do anything that would shatter this essential environment. The quickest way to lose both trust and respect is to make the things shared with you public or to use them for personal gain. A mentor who keeps confidences is a mentor that will claim the trust of their protégés.

Rule 5 - Seek to Broaden Understanding. Contrary to the widespread belief that a mentor is supposed to tell their protégé what to do as a leader, their actual job is to help their protégés learn how to think like a leader. Help those you are working with to broaden their understanding of correct leadership principles and allow them to draw their own conclusions on how to apply those principles. Good questions asked by a mentor are more powerful than good directions because the conclusions are drawn by the person with the most at stake. These experiences of self-discovery last far longer than a lecture, which is a far easier route for you as a mentor. Don't take the easy way out. If you can measure your success as a mentor by well thought out decisions made by your protégé rather than the facts and stories they memorize, you will be doing them a great and long term service in their careers and lives.

Whether you are being mentored or mentoring others, it is a powerful opportunity to grow. The greatest leaders have always understood this. The key is to be humble and embrace the experience. The leadership revolution will take a fuller effect as you treat the opportunity as invaluable, whether you are helping others to progress or accepting the help from someone you wish to emulate.

Who Are You and Who Are You Not?

If you walk like a duck, talk like a duck, in every way act like a duck, and choose to look like a duck, you will probably be viewed as a duck. On the same level, even if you are dishonest, you can speak like you are honest, look like you are honest, and act like you are honest, but you are still dishonest. Eventually the truth will come out, as it has for so many, and your real self will be revealed. What will people see? It is entirely up to you.

Living a lie will destroy you from the inside out. Living an honest life, at home and at work, will lead to a path that yields greater peace, greater confidence, and greater success. The worst liars are the ones who mix their lies with truth. This is the first step in rationalization, which leaders should always guard themselves against, not just from others, but from themselves. Let us share two powerful stories.

Living a Lie: A young man worked for the United Kingdom's oldest merchant bank as a derivatives broker. As he began to grow in the company, he began to take risks not approved by his superiors. His confidence was strong but unwarranted. Essentially he lied to himself about who he became in his short time as a broker. He lied to himself about his own capabilities and he lied to himself about his justifications in breaking procedures.

At first he found extreme financial success. That lasted a short time and the losses started piling up, all of which he lied about and hid from his bosses. Less than two years later, he lost the company over 300 million dollars, bankrupt one of Britain's oldest companies, and landed himself in prison. One lie started it all, and his once promising career spiraled into disaster.

Living with Honesty: Former Senator Larry Pressler is a man held in high regard not just for his political savvy and obvious intelligence. He may be best known for making national news with his deep commitment to honesty, even when it appeared as if no one else was watching.

Pressler, a Vietnam veteran, Oxford Rhodes Scholar, and Harvard Law School graduate, was a three term senator out of his home state of South Dakota. In 1980, while serving his one term in the House of Representatives, the FBI set up an undercover sting operation meant to investigate, tempt, and expose any corrupt U.S.

political officials by posing as an overseas company willing to exchange cash for political favors. Pressler stood alone as a champion of honesty. In a February 4, 1980 front page article in the Washington Post it was written,

"Thanks to the FBI's undercover "sting" operation, there now exists incontrovertible evidence that one senator would not be bought. Preserved among the videotape footage that may be used as bribery evidence against a number of members of Congress, there is a special moment in which Sen. Larry Pressler (R-SD) tells the undercover agents, in effect, to take their sting and stick it. Pressler, according to law enforcement sources was the one approached member of Congress who flatly refused to consider financial favors in exchange for legislative favors, as suggested by undercover agents... At the time he said he was not aware that he was doing anything quite so heroic,"

In a review of the FBI's actions and subsequent case, Judge J. Pratt is quoted as saying,"Pressler, particularly, acted as citizens have a right to expect their elected representatives to act. He showed a clear awareness of the line between proper and improper conduct, and despite his confessed need for campaign money, and despite the additional attractiveness to him of the payment offered, he nevertheless refused to cross into impropriety."

The two stories are not only polar opposites, but perfect examples of knowing who you are and who you are not. Living a lie is a misstatement. It is impossible to live only one lie, as it is always a series of lies, often piled upon each other over years. Knowing you are living an honest life will lead to a state where you will never need to fear who's watching you, what you've said to others, or how you perceive yourself. Honesty is not just the best policy, but the only policy that should be associated with the life of a leader.

Answer these three questions in any way you would like:

Who are you?

_____

_____

_____

_____

_____

_____

_____

_____

_____

Who are you not?

_____

_____

_____

_____

_____

_____

_____

_____

_____

_____

_____

Who are you going to be from now on?

_____

_____

_____

_____

_____

_____

_____

_____

_____

_____

_____

Set Your Values

Knowing who you are starts with the values you hold. We hear much of corporate values, or a set of rules and beliefs by which an organization abides by. Value statements are a proclamation of guiding principles by which a team member is expected to make decisions by and conduct themselves on a daily basis. Often, these are reflected within a simple list of values a company finds most important in meeting their goals and developing their people. For example, let's look at the Coca- Cola Company, an organization that was founded in 1886 and grew to be one of the largest international brands to ever exist. Their vision statement is simple but effective.

"Live Our Values"

\- Coca Cola

Our values serve as a compass for our actions and describe how we behave in the world.

1. **Leadership:** The courage to shape a better future.
2. **Collaboration:** Leverage collective genius.
3. **Integrity:** Be real.
4. **Accountability:** If it is to be, it's up to me.
5. **Passion:** Committed in heart and mind.
6. **Diversity:** As inclusive as our brands.
7. **Quality:** What we do, we do well.

Perfect. Since it's short, it's easy to break it down. First, notice the word compass, an indication that these values are a guiding light, a north star, by which to base decisions off of. How do team members know they are successful Coca-Cola employees? Only if they ARE actively doing things such as collaborating to "leverage collective genius," and promoting diversity "as inclusive as their brands." Next, let's look at the second key word, live. They did not use ground, memorize, strive for, or intend. Since 1/3 of your 24 hours is spent asleep and 1/3 is spent at work, it is crucial to decide on how you will live each day, as in this case, it will likely shape the course of your career. So how can employees at Coca-Cola make day-to-day decisions? By asking themselves things such as, "Am I really committed to this decision with both my heart and my mind?" If the answer is yes, (and ethical), do it! If the answer is no, they might ask themselves, "What can I change about these circumstances to really get behind it with passion?" Then, they make their decision based off that established guidance. We will talk more about these crucial value statements in another chapter, but first let's talk about you.

There is one problem with organizational value statements that we see over and over again. They are often created before, or without, people having the chance to create their own personal value statements. The Irish politician, Edmund Burke, made a remarkable comment some three centuries ago saying, "All that is necessary for the triumph of evil is that good men do nothing." We would add good women as well! Many a poor, and even illegal decision, has been made under the banner of believing, "I was just doing it for the good of the company." This is a trap no leader should fall into. You are accountable not only for the things you personally do and don't do, but also what you choose to turn a blind eye to.

In order to avoid this trap, and its devastating consequences, we employ the "I Will Never and I Will Always" technique. Essentially, what this does is create a code of conduct based on a value statement which you promise yourself you will always follow. This is meant to supersede even the value statement of your organization because without that fire of passion and self-peace burning within you, it will be hard to get behind any organizational decree. It is best to review these statements weekly.

It could easily look something like this....

"God first, family second, work third."

In regards to work, this could be an example of a guiding light.

The Allazo Group

My Value Statement: In my quest to fulfill the organization's mission, I will abide by the highest principles of my conscience and conduct myself with integrity as clearly defined in my "I Will Never and I Will Always" document. Here is an example:

I Will Never
- Lie, even if it makes me look bad.
- Step over another for personal gain.
- Do anything or say anything that will ruin my peer's ability to trust me.
- Let my self-worth, productivity, or my integrity, rise and fall with the opinions of those who do not really know me.
- Intentionally be late or belittle
- Boast of my own abilities or accomplishments.
- Engage in gossip or mindless arguments.
- Let my pride get in the way of the right decision.
- Stop choosing to learn.
- Create barriers that disrupt the overall mission of my team.

I Will Always
- Do my best, no matter what the task at hand.
- Be the same person in front of my subordinates as I am in front of my superiors.
- Communicate with others with respect and class.
- Remember that integrity is far more important than reputation.
- Consider the views of others and encourage their talents.
- Surround myself with those of integrity.
- Emulate the behavior I expect out of my fellow leaders, both in word and deed.
- Stand up for what I believe to be right.

No matter what your document contains, remember without integrity, your leadership is of no worth. The famed CEO of Berkshire Hathaway, Warren Buffet, taught about his personal motto in hiring leaders. "In looking for people to hire, look for three qualities: integrity, intelligence, and energy. And if they don't have the first one, the other two will kill you." Living a life without being true to your own integrity will certainly lead to devastation.

Your Values Document- Remember this is just a start!

I Will Never

-
-
-
-
-
-
-
-

I Will Always

-
-
-
-
-
-
-
-

The Power of Goals

To switch gears in the importance of becoming, there is a whole new level of power essential to the process that we have mentioned, but have yet to explore in depth. Both crucial and transforming, goals are key to leadership success.

Yet, few really understand the power of goals. They are what keep us motivated. They are what we have engraved on our minds when we put in extra effort to accomplish those things we find essential to our success at work and in life. It is more than just envisioning outcomes, but clear paths to getting there. As a leader, there are some impressive reasons to encourage goal setting and for you to set goals yourself. Consider this research:

In a study funded by the United Kingdom's Economic and Social Research Council (ESRC), in July 2015, the University of Leicester found that people who set goals have better focus and complete their tasks quicker than those who have no goals. The study was comprised of 109 participants who were asked to complete a simple addition problem of adding up sets of five, random two-digit numbers over five minutes' time. The participants were divided into three groups: in the control group, no goal was given. In the low group, they were given a goal of getting 10 correct answers. In the high group, their goal was 15 correct answers. The results showed participants in groups given goals had more correct answers and attempted more questions than the control group. In addition, there was not much difference between the high and low goal groups, proving that simply having a goal is effective by itself, regardless of how lofty the target.

By far, one of the most famous researchers of motivation and goal theories is Edwin A. Locke, a retired Dean's Professor of Motivation and Leadership at the Robert H. Smith School of Business at the University of Maryland, College Park. Through his studies, which have been endorsed by the American Psychological Association, Inc. as well as countless academics, he concludes that measurable, concrete goals are highly effective in performance improvement. To quote him, *"A review of both laboratory and field studies on the effects of setting goals when performing a task found that in 90% of the studies, specific and challenging goals lead to higher performance than easy goals, "do your best" goals, or no goals. Goals affect performance by directing attention, mobilizing effort, increasing persistence, and motivating strategy development."*

A goal can be an evolving force, and it is something we are about to discuss, but to really understand the power of goals, you need to first have the desire to progress, to get a little better, as well as to do a little more. When you have that desire, you are ready to harness that power and turn it into action. It is the equivalent of jumping two or three steps at a time on the spiral staircase upward.

Most of us have heard the acronym "SMART" in referring to goals. If you haven't or you have forgotten, here is your free MBA class for the day:

S- Specific   The goal needs to be detailed and not vague. An example would be; I will lose ten pounds as opposed to just "I will lose weight".

M- Measurable You need to be able to tell if the goal worked. Did I lose ten pounds or did I lose nine? There is a difference, and it can be measured.

A- Achievable   This part is key. Nothing is impossible, as the saying goes, but as far as goals go, there is only so much in your control. If my goal is for my friend to lost ten pounds, that is not an achievable goal on your part. You may support them, eat healthy with them, jog with them but ultimately, it is up to them.

R- Realistic   Unrealistic goals are sometimes met. There is power in not knowing what's impossible, but in the case of the normal, goals need to be something that can actually happen. Wanting to naturally lose 50 pounds in a week is unrealistic. Wanting to lose 50 pounds in a year is more realistic.

T- Timed   What is your deadline? Don't set a goal saying, "I want to lose 10 pounds.... eventually." Instead, pick a time frame and stick to it. One month, six months, eight? Whatever works for you as long as you can meet your own deadline.

This is an excellent way to set goals. Of course you want to be specific in what you are trying to accomplish. Of course you want to be able to measure those realistic results. In fact, it's a road map, and as J.R.R. Tolkien once expressed, "not all who wander are lost". This means that there are many who do wander who are lost. As Yogi Berra, the legendary and outspoken baseball catcher, said, "If you don't know where you're going, you'll end up someplace else." Goals should be SMART in nature. There is a reason the acronym has stood the test of time.

At The Allazo Group, we talk about the Four Levels of Goal Setting to go beyond the SMART acronym, or at least to bring it to life. Our desire is for you to develop into a Level Four goal setter and to be able to teach others around you how to be a Level Four goal setter. Let's go through them.

Level 0: No level at all. Thoughts, perhaps, but mostly these people will take what life gives them. Again, not a level, and no where you want to be.

Level 1: It's a start. Your goals are merely wishes. They are general at best. You may think about them often, but there is no concrete or even imagined plan behind them. Rarely do these work out, for they are left to chance, while being in the right place at the right time, without even knowing that's the case. Level 1 goal setters rarely see progress in meaningful ways as far as ambition and often look back on their years only to realize that the "one day" they hoped for never actually came.

For example, there was a man in his late twenties who constantly stated he had a goal to be a movie star, but he lived far away from Hollywood, and did not have any plans to move. He did not study acting, he did not look for auditions, as well as he did not reach out to people in the industry for advice. The farthest his planning went was to occasionally tell people he would be a movie star. The chances of success are extremely low, and somehow, that feels generous.

Level 2: These goal setters are focused. In their mind, they know what they want. It is specific, and it is thought about often. It is thought about so much that it's on their mind constantly. Level 2 goal setters are often found in the fiery determination of toddlers.

They want a new toy, they may not know what it takes to get it, but they are going to take whatever opportunities come their way to make it a reality.

A good example of a level two goal setter is a four-year-old boy who one of the authors has the privilege of knowing. While he is not quite at the point in his preschool education where there is much differentiation in money, he works tirelessly to try and earn "coins," pennies, dimes, quarters, it doesn't matter. His goal is to be able to buy, with the help of his mom and with his coins, a piece of candy for every member of his 20 student preschool class. He is often found asking his Mom for the jobs he can do for coins, or asking his grandparents if he could rake leaves (to which there were perhaps 50 in the whole yard) for coins. These tasks took him hours and more than a pint of determination, but over time, he accomplished his goal.

Being four, it is expected that his route to accomplishing his goal may not have been conventional, or even the fastest. However, though there was no timetable and a lack of efficiency, there was determination and an unwavering commitment to take any opportunity to bring him closer to his goal.

Level 3: These are excellent goal setters. The kind of goal setter our four-year-old friend will likely be by the age of 12. Not only do these goal setters have a very specific destination in mind, they also have their goals broken down into attainable benchmarks they can achieve along the way. They prioritize and write out their goals, keeping them where they can see them on a daily, or even an hourly basis. They realize Rome wasn't built overnight, but was built road by road, brick by brick, and these goal setters are conscious enough to realize the importance of each of these roads and each of these bricks in their ultimate plan.

One key jump from level two to level three is having your goals written down. A study conducted by Dr. Gail Mathews of The Dominican University of California found that there is a significant gap in the overall success between those who write down their goals versus those who simply keep their goals in their mind. In the words of former management professor, Michael Leboeuf, "When you write down your ideas you automatically focus your full attention on them. Few if any of us can write one thought and think another at the same time. Thus a pencil and paper make excellent concentration tools."

A good example of a level 3 goal setter is a man we have known for some time. He has succeeded in every venture in which he has endeavored and currently runs a highly successful tech company. Part of his secret to success is his deep commitment to goal setting. To him, it all starts with a vision. Often, he will retreat into a national park or another secluded destination and will make specific goals with specific plans for the next phase of his life, whether it be weeks or years. He will ask himself these questions, "What do I desire to happen?", "When do I desire it to happen by?", "What am I willing to sacrifice to make it happen?", "What are the obstacles that will keep this from happening?", And finally, "What specific steps do I need to take to make it happen?" He writes down the answers and modifies as needed while never varying from the core plan. His family has also participated in this exercise and from an outsider's perspective, their results have been remarkable.

Level 4: Level Four goal setters see the most success in their lives because they know how to design their existence in such a way

87

that success naturally follows. There are only a few key things that separate a Level 3 goal setter from a Level 4 goal setter, but they are a springboard to a higher sense of confidence and accomplishment. Like Level Three goal setters, Level 4 goal setters are fiercely determined to make their dreams a reality. Their attitude towards their desires is reflected in all they do. Thomas Jefferson observed, "Nothing can stop the man with the right mental attitude from achieving his goal; nothing on earth can help the man with the wrong mental attitude." Attitude is the key to overcoming the obstacles that come your way.

Level 4 goal setters do things that others simply don't think to do. Here are a few examples of the traits of a Level 4 goal setter.

- They read their goals out loud, daily.
- They have a daily goal that contribute to weekly or monthly goals that ultimately contribute to their overall goal.
- They don't believe in stretch goals, if they are going to have one goal and then another goal, they don't see the sense in having the first goal at all.
- They visualize and even write down what their life, career, attitude, etc. will be like when their goal is accomplished.
- They talk in terms of when and not "if" with no shame.
- They don't procrastinate beginning.
- They don't take days off.
- Their motivation never falters.
- They have others hold them accountable.

We imagine the Wright Brothers, the founders of flight, as being amazing examples of Level 4 goal setters. They started with the assumption of when and not if. It took years to get their first plane into the air but day in and day out they worked under the premise, "If we worked on the assumption that what is accepted as true really is true, then there would be little hope for advance." Their motivation never faltered, even as they were mocked and ridiculed for what seemed to be an impossible dream. We can deduce that aviation was the topic of countless conversations and being in a partnership, they held each other accountable to do the things necessary to keep their goal alive. Steps were taken, small ones maybe, but every day to contribute to their overall goal, not to glide, not to lift off, but to fly. Today thousands of flights take off and land across the world. The Wright Brothers literally connected the world in a previously unimaginable way and changed the course of human history. All of this, which may even be understating their impact, was because they abided by the discipline and principles of Level 4 goal setters.

What Level Four Goal setters do you know? What sets them apart in your mind?

_____

_____

_____

_____

_____

_____

_____

_____

_____

What level of goal setter are you? What do you need to do TODAY to start making the move to the next level or to stay at a Level 4?

_____

_____

_____

_____

_____

_____

_____

_____

_____

_____

_____

What steps will you take to become a Level 4 goal setter in the next six months? Be as S.M.A.R.T. as possible!

_____

_____

_____

_____

_____

_____

_____

_____

_____

_____

_____

Wrapping It Up

The process of becoming is a never ending process but it should also be a joyous process in the life and career of every leader. The more you become, the more capacity you have to do good in your organization, in your home, and in the world. Complacency, even when times are good, is the enemy to progress. Don't mistake activity for effectiveness. Look deeply into your values, your mission, your goals, and become not only what you want to become, but what you must become! The process of becoming is the spark that lights the flame that illuminates the path to the rest of the Leadership Revolution. Like a fire, that illumination will only increase when added to. If ignored, it will slowly drift into abyss. Forward or backwards, when it comes to becoming, there is no standing still.

EMPOWER

The Essence of Empowerment

Cesar Chavez, by his own admonition, had no interest in politics. He, like his parents before him, took up the profession of migrant farming. In his time working up and down the state of California with the different seasons of crops, he witnessed first-hand the obscenity in the treatment of the Mexican- American population contracted to work the fields. Pesticide was dropped on their heads, getting out of a crouched position when doing a day's work of picking was penalized and often cruel foreman would beat and belittle their inferiors.

In this backdrop Cesar Chavez found himself, like so many great leaders before him, in the very turnings of the leadership revolution. Through his own study, experiences, and observations, he had made the applications necessary to become a leader. When asked by his peers to lead a cause greater than himself, he was the most instrumental figure in the history of farm workers' rights, bringing what now seem basic human dignities in the way of reform to the farming industry. Cesar Chavez understood the wisdom of empowering others better than about anyone. One principle he taught over and over again, summarizes the Allazo Group's feelings behind empowerment. "You cannot organize the masses until you have organized the individual." Time and time again, this was the motto by which Chavez lived, taking ordinary people in ordinary communities and helping them see their worth, their talents, and their unique contribution to the cause of farm worker's rights.

Everything we have talked about up until this point has been about empowering yourself. The next step in the leadership revolution, the next step in the ascension to the pantheon of highly effective leadership is to take what you have become and use your leadership to masterfully empower others.

Empowering others, at its core, means helping others to see their potential, reach their potential, and use that realized potential to contribute to the good of the organization and to the good of their lives. Empowerment speaks to the human soul. As human beings, we crave it. When we see it, it touches us deeply. Examples of empowerment are all around us, which should be no surprise as it is the second step in the Leadership Revolution, timeless in its very nature. Let's explore some lasting examples from the movies and novels of empowering others, the themes are as applicable as the stories are memorable. See if you gain that feeling of connection we're talking about.

Movies

- Remember the Titans: In this iconic film the true story of T.C. Williams High School is retold through the lens of the newly integrated football team and their first year head coach, Herman Boone. Boone, a black teacher, at this successful, formerly all-white powerhouse football oriented school, becomes an inspiring and empowering figure despite seemingly insurmountable obstacles. He not only preaches teamwork, respect and vision, but puts his players in a position to discover these profound traits for themselves. Despite obstacles, the team overcomes the stereotypes of the 1960's en route to winning a championship as a united family.

- Freedom Writers: The true story of Erin Gruwell, an enthusiastic yet new teacher who left her comfortable hometown of Newport Beach to teach English at Woodrow Wilson High School in the heart of Long Beach. Her lack of tenure leads her to teaching a group of kids, essentially given up on by the system. Coming from the roughest backgrounds this young teacher had seen and divided into racially segregated groups, Gruwell struggles to make any kind of connection with her students. Relentless and capitalizing on making real world connections in the classroom her students can relate to in their lives, she ultimately wins their trust and empowers them to tell their own story in the way of a groundbreaking book. Ultimately, through her influence she inspires every student in her original sophomore class to tell their own story as opposed to the story society would tell about them and graduate from high school.

- The Sandlot: It's hard to question the leadership of Benny "the Jet" Rodriguez, a young baseball prodigy and leader of the Sandlot gang. With no uniforms, no money and no real "Field" to play on, Benny manages to empower his fellow teammates to reach their full potential simply through leading by example. His passion for the game, his loyalty to his teammates and his acceptance and mentoring of the less than talented "Smalls" doesn't go unnoticed. Benny refuses to draw attention to himself but instead lives his empowering lifestyle without the fanfare that he has deservedly earned. In true empowering fashion, as he rose in maturity and skill, everyone around him rose with him.

- Twelve O'clock High: Some would argue that 12 O'clock High is THE definitive movie about leadership. Period. In any case, it's an incredible story of an empowering leader and an empowered team. In this WWII film revolving around an American bombing unit fallen into chaos due to poor leadership, an officer named General Savage is brought in to bring a sense of order and success to this group of ragtag men. To empower his men he firsts breaks them down; breaks down their pride, breaks down their habits, breaks down everything they thought they knew about flying a bombing mission. Though the men's very lives are at stake they rebel against Savage and his tactics. Savage, not caring about his popularity doesn't ease up for a minute. His men over time are empowered by his example, come to respect him deeply and transform their service into the ultimate example of what an American Air Unit was supposed to look like.

Novels

- To Kill a Mockingbird: Atticus Finch, a single father in the deep south in the early 1930's was the only lawyer willing to defend an African- American accused of a crime it was clear he didn't commit. His children were ridiculed and Atticus himself put his own life on the line standing up for what was right, despite popular opinion and deep rooted prejudices. Atticus's compassion and fairness were attributes he developed over a lifetime and his example to his children and community changed lives and hearts as he unequivocally stood up against injustice and intolerance in every form. Atticus walked the path alone at first, but became a champion of hope and justice, especially in his own home. The late Harper Lee, writing this novel in a racially charged America, herself became a catalyst in changing the views of countless people around the world.

- Charlotte's Web: Charlotte, a common farm spider, realized her life on earth was short and decided to devote much of it to empowering a young pig named Wilbur who finds himself alone and near slaughtering at Mr. Zuckerman's farm. Through Charlotte's guidance, Wilbur's life is not only spared but he becomes a celebrity in the local community. After Charlotte's passing Wilbur returns the favor by empowering Charlotte's children and subsequent posterity for the rest of his rich and abundant life.

- A Christmas Carol: Ebenezer Scrooge knew nothing but a life of heartache, a thirst for money and a desire to make those around him as miserable as himself. Through the visit of three angels, his eyes are opened to his own ability to do good, the real purpose of life and the truth that his career was such a small part of who he was as a human being. He turned his view outward and spent the rest of his life building others, giving of his time and wealth and setting the example in the great city of London of philanthropy and kind heartedness.

- The Sign of Four: The rebirth of sorts of Sherlock Holmes and his sidekick Dr. Watson is filled with brilliant leadership insights. Despite Sherlock's incredible skills of deduction, Dr. Watson brings out the leadership skills of Holmes through keeping him grounded, keeping him focused and helping his fill in blanks by being a capable listener and counselor. Through their adventures, Holmes teaches the power of logic and common sense in leadership and that one must work to excel in any endeavor and that knowledge, opposed to hearsay, holds power.

There is a reason that movies and books like these and countless others resonate with us. They speak to our soul. As human beings, we know we are not on this world alone, we have an innate desire to empower others to the greatness we strive for ourselves. These movies host the role models that manifest what we strive to be as empowering leaders and they the miracles in people's lives that come when empowered. Take notes as you watch movies revolving around empowering leaders. Their lessons are as real as they are endless.

What is a movie or novel that has taught you a powerful lesson on empowering others? Why was it so impactful?

_____

_____

_____

_____

_____

_____

_____

_____

Never Set Limitations On Who Can Be Empowered to Do Great Things

Long ago, we heard one of the many fascinating stories told of the famed Swiss-American Biologist, Louis Agassiz. As the story goes, the Harvard Professor of the 1800's was lecturing in London and he drew a large and passionate crowd. A fiery little old lady, but one who did not seem to have much money or luxury associated with her life, came up and was spiteful to say the least. She was resentful and said she had never had the chances he had had and she hoped he appreciated it. He took that bit of a scourge very pleasantly and turned to the lady and, when she was through, said, "What do you do?"

She said, "I run a boarding house with my sister. I'm unmarried."

"What do you do at the boarding house?"

"Well, I skin potatoes and chop onions for the stew. We have stew every day."

"Where do you sit when you do that interesting but homely task?"

"I sit on the bottom step of the kitchen stairs."

"Where do your feet rest when you sit there on the bottom step?"

"On a glazed brick."

"What is a glazed brick?"

"I don't know."

"How long have you been sitting there?"

"Fifteen years."

Agassiz concluded, "Here's my card. Would you write me a note when you get a moment about what a glazed brick is?"

Well that made her mad enough to go home and do it. She went home and got the dictionary out and found out that a brick was a piece of baked clay. That didn't seem enough to send to a Harvard professor, so she went to the encyclopedia and found out that a brick was made of vitrified kaolin and hydrous aluminum silicate, which didn't mean a thing to her. She went to work and visited a brick factory and a tile maker. Then she went back in history and studied a little bit about geology and learned something about clay and clay beds and what *hydrous* meant and what *vitrified* meant. She began to soar out of the basement of a boarding house on the wings of words like *vitrified kaolin* and *hydrous aluminum silicate*. She finally decided that there were about 120 different kinds of glazed bricks and tiles. She could tell Agassiz, so she wrote him a little note of thirty-six pages and said, "Here's your glazed brick."

He wrote back, "That is a fine piece of work. If you change this and that and the other, I'll prepare it for publication and send you that which is due you from publication." She thought no more of it, made the changes, sent it back, and almost by return mail came a check for 250 dollars. His letter said, "I've published your piece. What was under the brick?"

And she said, "Ants."

He replied (all of this by mail), "What's an ant?"

She went to work and this time she was excited. She found 1825 different kinds of ants. She found there were ants that you could put three to the head of a pin and still have standing room left over. She found that there were ants an inch long that moved in armies half a mile wide and destroyed everything in their path. She found that some ants were blind; some ants lost their wings on the afternoon they died; some milked cows and took the milk to the aristocrats up the street. She found more ants than anyone had ever found, so she wrote Mr. Agassiz something of a treatise, numbering 360 pages. He published it and sent her the money and royalties, which continued to come in. She saw the lands and places of her dreams on a little carpet of vitrified kaolin and on the wings of flying ants that may lose their wings on the afternoon they die.

In the words of Dr. Leo Buscaglia, "Too often we underestimate the power of a touch, a smile, a kind word, a listening ear, an honest compliment, or the smallest act of caring, all of which have the potential to turn a life around."

Who can you empower today?

_____

_____

_____

_____

_____

_____

Know Your People

We heard a story not long ago at a business conference for one of the great international universities. The story was of a man who loved Japan. He was an international director over the Japanese market for a large and prestigious North American accounting firm. When asked how many times he had been to Japan, he said, "8 times in the last year". And how long did you stay each time? "At least a week, and I loved every minute of it."

But as the conversation continued, some very interesting details began to emerge. For example, he was always immediately taken from the airport to his American chain hotel. From there he was picked up by American employees of the firm working in Japan. When he met with his Japanese coworkers, it was at a well-known American restaurant. He knew no Japanese, made no attempt at learning Japanese and during the week met only with those that spoke English, expecting them to relay his message down the line. After a few tourist attractions, he was on his way back to the States with a feeling of accomplishment and a suitcase full of souvenirs. In essence, this man spent 1/6th of his year in Japan but was never actually in "Japan". When push came to shove, he had the respect of five or six employees but little to no impact on the rest of the team he was charged to oversee. Profits declined and more and more pressure was put on local managers. This could be a problem linked to international management, but at its core it's a problem with not knowing your people well enough to make an actual difference.

Contrast that with these other true stories:

The CEO of a large corporation makes it her personal mission to know the names of every employee and their spouses from her vice presidents all the way down to the people in the maintenance office. She makes it her personal mission to send out a hand written thank you card to each employee each year.

A man who presides over a large organization keeps a book that contains the names and contact information of each of his employees. Under the contact information, he writes down what he knows about his employees; birthdays, interests, life goals, etc. Though his team is spread out across the country, he studies his book and when given the opportunity to talk to a team member, he uses the information he gathers as a reference point and makes special note to write down any new information he gains because he knows in the long run it makes all the difference not just in hs effectiveness but in the lives of those he leads.

An owner of a tiny restaurant employs at risk teenagers. She makes it a point to mentor them and no what's going on in their lives. She knows them well enough to where they come to her for advice. One day one of her waiters walks in late with an angry look on his face. She immediately knows he has been in an argument with his girlfriend (again) and is in no mood to serve. This restaurant owner is understanding but also firm, before the young man can say anything, she says "You are in no position to serve anyone here because you did not leave your problem at the door. Go out and try again." The young man, leaves the restaurant, gathers himself and has a successful shift.

The President and Director of an organization consisting of thousands of members hears word that one of his newly promoted managers was taking the day off because he had worked through the night trying to move his pregnant wife and two very young children into their new home by himself. He hadn't made it very far. The president of the company unexpectedly showed up at his manager's door in work clothes. The manager was shocked and asked his boss, "What are you doing here? Did I miss something at work? I thought I had everything in order." The president of the company just smiled and said, "Everything is fine. If you can take the day off, I can too." He immediately started grabbing boxes and carrying them into the house. He stayed until the family was fully moved in that night.

In your mind, what is the difference between the first story and the following four stories? What principles do you think you can apply today to your leadership?

_____
_____
_____
_____
_____
_____
_____
_____
_____
_____
_____
_____
_____
_____
_____

Quickly, name those you work with and what you really know about them? What would you like to know about them? How can you serve them? What atmosphere can you create to know them better as individuals and fellow passengers up the Revolution?

_____
_____

_____
_____
_____
_____
_____
_____
_____
_____
_____
_____
_____
_____
_____
_____
_____
_____
_____
_____
_____
_____
_____
_____
_____

Mission and Vision - Irreplaceable

Organizationally, do we really know where we are going? If all roads in the ancient world led to Rome, then equally all roads certainly need to lead back to the fundamental mission of your organization. Rome was the center of civilization; the mission statement is the center of your organization. This is crucial. Mission and people, people and mission, they have to go hand in hand.

A mission statement is a one sentence declaration of why an organization exists. It is the WHY behind your organization's actions. Along with your values, it is the declaration of what you stand for day in and day out. It should be referred to over and over. It should not only be memorized but believed, not just recited but lived.

Here is an example worth noting. The Kellogg Company has an excellent day in and day out mission statement, "Nourishing families so they can flourish and thrive." Simple, direct, and not a destination but a path towards a destination. When asked what they do at the Kellogg company? Nourish families so they can flourish. How do they do it? By providing quality products families need to be physically nourished. So for the Kellogg company, what is the end destination? Their corporate vision which is "To enrich and delight the world through foods and brands that matter."

A vision statement is the destination and the mission statement is how you get there. The greater you and your team understand AND practice these two guiding statements, the more likely you are to progress upward in the leadership revolution.

A company's vision statement could easily be called a "What Do We Need to Become to Fulfill Our Mission Statement". Without a clear understanding of what your organization needs to become, it will be hard for your team to envision the success *you* already see in the future. When people not only see the vision but share the vision of the course of the company or organization, they will be inspired, lifted and excited. One of the greatest opportunities and responsibilities of a leader is to help people create, see, buy in and implement a united vision.

A vision statement is a declaration to yourself and the world of where you are going and what you will be. All plans in the organization can be directly linked back to this fundamental "X" at the end of the map. Trying to plan before having a vision is about as useful as trying to find the New York Harbor while driving around the state of Minnesota.

The first steps in creating an accepted vision, is to have a little vision. Where do you see yourself and your organization at the end of five years? Some find it helpful to put this in a story, others like to talk about the facts that will exist in five years. No matter what your strategy, putting pencil to paper is the first step in really organizing the chaos of what could be into the vision of what will be.

So can you simply define what you want your organization, or even you, to be in five years or even five minutes? We find the vision of Microsoft helpful and inspiring. "A computer on every desktop." How simple is that? If you were leading Microsoft, you could easily stand up and say, "Our vision or where we are going to be in three years is simple. We will have a computer on every desktop." Does this give the marketing department clear direction? Yes. Does this give research and development a clear direction? Yes. Does this give manufacturing a clear direction? Absolutely.

Empower Others Through Your Own Mission and Vision

As you become, your actions will be observed by others and inspire others. In the leadership revolution there comes a certain step where you cannot progress without articulating the mission of your life and a vision or roadmap on how you are going to continually get there. Not only will this empower you but it is an almost certainty that your commitment to your mission and vision will inspire those around you.

Set the example by creating your own one to two sentence personal mission statement as well as a short but detailed vision statement. Empower others to do the same. The direction and inspiration these statements give to people are invaluable.

You may feel the need to create multiple mission and vision statements for different aspects of your life. That's great! Make sure that every one of them, no matter how different, align with your values statement. Without that detail, your world will continually feel out of balance.

Here are a few examples:

Personal Mission Statements:

To be honest and true to everyone I meet.

To lead, inspire and innovate at every opportunity.

Always be one step ahead of our key markets, focusing on the future while executing today.

Personal Vision Statements:

To leave a legacy of service that will be remembered when I leave this world.

To be a world class leader respected by myself and others for their innovative and forward thinking.

To have my actions in the classroom help thousands of students to be productive members of society.

As others see you living, revising and living your personal mission and vision statements, you will be in the perfect position to empower those around you. Like snowflakes falling from a winter's sky, no one's statements will be the same. That is just fine!! Diversity is a powerful tool, especially when you take into account human intelligence (as mentioned before) and human character are the most powerful of the twenty first century business currencies.

Mission and Vision of Notable Companies

Here are some examples of the personal mission statements of three well known CEO's.

"To live life with integrity and empathy, and be a positive force in the lives of others."

- Amy Ziari, CEO of the noted marketing consulting group, Pasta

"To serve as a leader, live a balanced life, and apply ethical principles to make a significant difference."

- Denise Morrison, CEO of the Campbell Soup Company

"To have fun in my journey and learn from my mistakes."

- Sir Richard Branson, Founder of the Virgin Group

And then mission statements of some well-known companies.

"To be earth's most customer-centric company; to build a place where people can come to find and discover anything they might want to buy online."

- Amazon

"To safely market and distribute energy and petrochemical products while offering innovative value in added services."

- Royal Dutch Shell

"To organize the world's information and make it universally accessible and useful."

- Google

For good measure, the vision statements of some well-known companies.

"GM's vision is to be the world leader in transportation products and related services. We will earn our customers' enthusiasm through continuous improvement driven by the integrity, teamwork, and innovation of GM people."

- GM

The AT&T global network was born of the ingenuity of AT&T Labs networking specialists who made disparate systems work together. Being the world's fastest and most reliable global network, our network is the standard against which all others are measured. To maintain our leadership in this arena, we focus on the future and aggressively pursue innovations. Our vision is to design and create in this decade the new global network, processes, and service platforms that maximize automation, allowing for a reallocation of human resources to more complex and productive work.

- AT&T

"We believe that we are on the face of the earth to make great products and that's not changing. We are constantly focusing on innovating. We believe in the simple not the complex. We believe that we need to own and control the primary technologies behind the products that we make, and participate only in markets where we can make a significant contribution. We believe in saying no to thousands of projects, so that we can really focus on the few that are truly important and meaningful to us. We believe in deep collaboration and cross-pollination of our groups, which allow us to innovate in a way that others cannot. And frankly, we don't settle for anything less than excellence in every group in the company, and we have the self-honesty to admit when we're wrong and the courage to change. And I think regardless of who is in what job those values are so embedded in this company that Apple will do extremely well."

- Apple Inc. According to CEO, Tim Cook

To review, a vision statement is the destination. The purpose statement is the fundamental purpose that gets you up every morning and guides you to that destination. Your values keep you on the road and steering clear of self-inflicted roadblocks. The three together create a powerful force for organizational success.

What Really Motivates People

What really motivates people? Without looking at the list below, write in what you think are the real motivation of people working in organizations across the world.

1.
2.
3.
4.
5.

Here are some common survey responses, how many of them ended up on your list?

1. Money
2. Prestige
3. Bigger and better things; houses, cars, etc.
4. Fear of looking bad in front of others
5. Fear of failure
6. Bonuses

These make sense right? But the truth is they are wrong. Or at least they are short term motivations at best. Daniel Pink, author of Drive: The Surprising Truth About What Motivates Us does a masterful job of taking the science and research behind human motivation and contrasting that with what businesses and other organization's actually do. The differences are night and day.

True motivation is intrinsic. It comes from the power to create and follow one's passions, to master their craft with autonomy and purpose. It has to come from within and the best thing a leader can do is to create opportunities for that intrinsic purpose to flourish. External motivations are fine when coupled with what really matters but standing alone are simply a practice of the old guard.

Two quotes from Pink's book we think every leader should know by heart:

"Human beings have an innate inner drive to be autonomous, self-determined, and connected to one another. And when that drive is liberated, people achieve more and live richer lives."

"The problem with making an extrinsic reward the only destination that matters is that some people will choose the quickest route there, even if it means taking the low road. Indeed, most of the scandals and misbehavior that have seemed endemic to modern life involve shortcuts."

So how do we create the kind of atmosphere within our organizations that allow this kind of success to flourish? Here are a few ideas that are directly tied to the Revolution:

1. Help people find their purpose in life AND in work. If a clear sense of purpose is both seen and felt on a daily basis it will directly respond with motivation and an inner burning to succeed.
2. Help people to feel free to do things because they want to and not because management says they have to.
3. Do everything in your power to empower those around you to discover their talents and embrace them.

4. Put people in positions where their talents can flourish!

Fill out this chart after talking with your employees, see if there is a logical change that can be made for the benefit of the individual and the organization.

What do they excel at?	
What is their passion?	
Where do the two align in your organization to create the best fit?	

Empowering people is motivating people. Empowering well means helping others to motivate themselves through their own passions and desire to be fulfilled in their work. You can simply be a guide and watch as you and everyone around you moves up step by step on the revolution.

Note: Do you feel unfulfilled at work? It might not be a bad idea and fill out this chart for yourself!

What do YOU excel at?	
What is YOUR passion?	
Where do the two align in your organization to create the best fit?	

Everyone Empowered

Empowerment is a principle best shared equally. Everyone from senior management down to summer intern feeling safe to succeed and supported in their role is a real hallmark of an effective organization. It is powerful when the only thing that matters is the success of the organization and not the relegating of team members to gratify one's own success. However, no one should get the idea that they are permitted to overstep their bounds. They should feel comfortable in openly expressing their opinions in appropriate settings and feel supported in becoming exceptional in their individual roles but never force themselves into the roles of others. There is a difference between feeling entitled and empowered.

When you feel entitled, you can quickly move from the realm of appropriate confidence to arrogance and a feeling that you *are* the company as opposed to being a *part* of the company. A recent example of this was a man in an organization who became so popular to those around him that he unwisely assumed his views represented the views of the entire brand. This went from a simple feeling to feeling entitled to speak with the press on behalf of the organization without any consultation to the public relations department, his senior management or even his common sense. This ultimately led to disaster as he took an interview, shooting from the hip and declaring his views on behalf of the organization that not only put him in a bad light but everyone around him as well. Furthermore, what he said was untrue of his organization and then taken even further out of context by the media, putting the public relations department into an impossible situation.

Empowered people act differently. Empowered people act with confidence in their own abilities but feel much of their strength coming from their organization. They have enough self confidence and trust built up over time that they find no need to backbite, fear or ridicule others. They are positive and team first, knowing their role and realizing that they are not a one man (or woman) band. They take responsibility for their own growth and happiness while finding fulfillment in what they do every day to contribute to the success of the organization.

As a leader, one of your crucial roles is to empower those around you. There are countless ways to empower others, but the truth is that most leaders A. Don't develop the skill of empowering others, opting to use the same approaches over the course of a career and B. Only empower those closest to them. In the best organizations, EVERYONE feels empowered in their role as an individual and as a member of the team. This includes the night cleaning crew, the newly hired employees, the woman who is about to retire after 40 years of service, or the newly appointed vice president or assistant principal.

We think you should keep a list of effective empowerment strategies to avoid being trapped in the same approaches over and over. You are surrounded by individuals and every individual may very well need a different approach from you in order to feel empowered. The following are some simple empowerment strategies you can begin to apply today to develop your personnel and ignite their confidence. Add to the list as you begin to apply these strategies.

- Confidence comes from success; success comes from the building blocks of the little wins often ignored. Help those around you to be successful in their roles by clearly communicating expectations and celebrating the little wins with them consistently.

- Encourage innovation and don't feel more loyalty to procedures and practices that you know can be improved than to those you are leading. Within each member of your organization is a universe of untapped potential, encourage them to harness those unique abilities for the betterment of the organization. Give an individual or a team a problem and let them use their imaginations and skill sets to solve the problem. You yourself will need to be open to new ways of thinking but you will find positive progress in promoting innovation.

- Give power to others by delegating responsibility. Show confidence in their abilities and encourage your team member in their efforts. Invite them to report back to you every day on their progress but let that time be a time of encouragement, not micro managing. It is amazing what people can accomplish when they feel empowered.

- _____
   _____
   _____
   _____
   _____
   _____

- _____
   _____
   _____
   _____
   _____
   _____

- _____
   _____
   _____
   _____
   _____
   _____

Your Positivity Matters

There is an old saying that one cannot ignore when hiking through the mountains or driving through a street with hanging oaks engulfing the sunlight. It is nearly impossible to measure the true effect one tree can have, because in the power of a single acorn lies the potential for an entire forest.

The same power lies in the leader who commits to a positive attitude. Not an unrealistic attitude, mind you, but a positive attitude. It's infectious just as much as a negative attitude. Science has proven it but so have our everyday experiences. For example, boss had bad argument with his neighbor, comes into a meeting the next day and begins eight hours of negative rhetoric towards his young assistant. She in turn is in a bad mood even though she had a great night out with her family the previous evening. She goes home to her husband with this bad mood, her kids pick up on it like only children can and in turn begin to act out the next day in school causing their teachers to feel overwhelmed and stressed.

Where did it start? No one can know for sure but the path from the neighbor to the teachers passed through a workplace and chances are most of these people have never met. Yet their attitude had a ripple effect even more powerful than their acquaintance! Now take that same principle, apply the law of attraction in a fishbowl that is a building that houses an organization and you can see how negative attitudes spread like wildfire.

Negativity doesn't just create discomfort, it is the breeding ground for worry and fear and the antithesis of safety and optimism. It is not simply a bad habit but a destructive practice that will infiltrate your organization and rot it from the inside out. In reality, only one attitude can exist within a person at a time and you as a leader have a disproportionate ability to establish what that attitude might be. Our suggestion is to empower your organization with a continual focus on the positive.

A focus on the positive is a focus on opportunity. When one is freed from worrying about their job, the reprimand they don't feel they deserve or the tyranny of an overbearing leader, they can turn their attention to things that matter, like maximizing the value, success and bottom line of the organization you share.

So it is your job to focus on the positive, not just because it's good for your health, not just because it is infectious but because it is statistically proven to breed success. It is a powerful way to empower. If you were to turn and look at something from the podium while addressing all the employees in your organization at the annual Holiday party, their natural reaction would be to follow your gaze. If you come in every day with a hardworking, positive attitude, their natural reaction will be to follow your example. In the words of the Dalai Lama, "In order to carry a positive action we must first create here a positive vision." Remove negativity at all costs but then don't leave that space empty, replace it with forward moving positivity. It is impossible to have a positive organization with consisting of leadership with a negative attitude.

Authenticity, Transparency and the Why

The why of a leader's actions is at the heart of transparency, but there are certain criteria that every leader needs to understand about transparency before they can be trusted in their motivations and reasoning. This is where authenticity makes its entrance.

In a 2005 Leadership Quarterly article, Boas Shamir and Galit Eilam put out four steps we have found crucial to leadership authenticity. They shared and listed, "the following four characteristics of authentic leaders: (1) rather than faking their leadership, authentic leaders are true to themselves (rather than conforming to the expectations of others); (2) authentic leaders are motivated by personal convictions, rather than to attain status, honors, or other personal benefits; (3) authentic leaders are originals, not copies (pp. xx); that is, they lead from their own personal point of view; and (4) the actions of authentic leaders are based on their personal values and convictions."

To understand authenticity better, let's analyze those four steps again a little closer.

- Authentic leaders are true to themselves: You can't try to be someone else. You can adopt their attitudes, habits and develop their strengths, but at the end of the day, you are still you. This is especially crucial in situations where one leader is taking over for another leader. If the first leader was successful, it will be tempting for the second leader to mimic everything the first leader did and was in order to keep up appearances. But this never really works. Organizations are meant to improve. Instead of being that leader, it is better to build on the foundation of that leader and let the organization grow and not simply stay stagnant.

- Authentic leaders are motivated by personal convictions: In Gandhi's words, "A NO uttered from the deepest conviction is better than a 'Yes' merely uttered to please, or worse, to avoid trouble." Without conviction, a leader will lack passion, and without passion there is no inspiration much less commitment. Belief must exist and that belief is best when it comes from the heart accompanied with the mind. A thought out course and a determined course. A course a leader follows not just because their corporate headquarters told them to but because at their very core, they want to.

- Authentic leaders are originals: Being original is the first step in being innovative. To accomplish things that haven't been seen in the past, we need to do things and see things differently in the future. Frank Lloyd Wright pioneered a new generation of architecture through his vision and commitment to his own creativity. His philosophy, "Every great architect is- necessarily- a great poet. He *must* be a great original interpreter of his time, his day, his age." There is the old adage that if it isn't broken you shouldn't fix it. In most cases, especially in procedures this applies splendidly. But we would also argue that the pianos on which Mozart, Beethoven and Bach orchestrated their masterpieces probably didn't have broken keys. Like your leadership they took a proven instrument and made it their own.

- Authentic leaders' actions are based on their personal values and convictions: This directly comes back to your values statement you created earlier in the book. If you skipped over that section now would be a good time to go back and do it! Without values, leadership is hollow. Your leadership, no matter how hard you try, will never be full without incorporation your personal values and convictions. You are not a machine. You are made up of heart, determination, a soul and countless experiences that have shaped you. To ignore those qualities is to ignore your greatest potential.

Why and transparency should go right in line with authenticity. When an employee or team member is constantly asking themselves why they are doing what they are doing, they are more productive and clear in their purpose. When a leader is there to answer the question of "Why" with complete transparency, the leaders and those being led can act in harmony.

As a leader you should always be prepared to answer the question of "Why." If a culture of asking "Why" is in place, the question's motivation will rarely be driven by anger or frustration but by a yearning for understanding as well as a drive to fulfill the purpose of the organization. In the "Why" you as a leader can make a compelling case for the reasons behind your actions and the bright future of your organization.

You are only a real leader based on the decisions of others, people need to choose to follow you. If they do not consciously choose to follow you, you may be a manager but never a true leader. This is most likely accomplished when there is transparency in your actions. If members of your organization are constantly questioning your motives, something has gone wrong. Does this mean you should share everything you are doing as a leader? No, that would likely be inappropriate more times than not. But there are some simple things you can do to create a more transparent style of leadership.

1. Share what you can. People love to be a part of things and appropriate information can go a long way. If you come back from a board meeting or a meeting with senior management and there is information you can share, don't hold back, share it.
2. Explain your reasoning behind decisions. People will appreciate your honesty and come closer to the "Why" faster than any other way. Have other leaders coming from other meetings do the same. Transparency in organization wise.
3. Use systems and information sharing software that allow for an open door, instantaneous sharing to take place from department to department.

As you create this kind of transparency, your actions will be questioned less, employee engagement will rise and teamwork will increase. People will understand their roles from multiple perspectives and will hopefully, cease to worry about the jobs of others. More than anything trust will be built AND sustained over time, allowing you, as the leader, to build something special along the way.

One on One with Leaders

One of our esteemed colleagues and college professor shared the following analogy and insights. We thought it to be more than appropriate to share as a way of conveying the importance of one on one leadership. The following section is in his words.

"The opportunity for people to meet with you one on one in non-threatening settings is a magnificent opportunity for empowerment. Let us lead you through some guided imagery. As you read, know that a crucial question will be asked of you at the end that you'll need to answer truthfully and with detail... Got it? Let's start.

Imagine yourself on vacation and in a fish market on a coastal city of your choice. You're on the docks, surrounded by people, seagulls, and most noticeably fish. Fish of all kinds, big fish, small fish, fat fish, skinny fish, smelly fish, even more smelly fish, every kind of fish you could ever want on a dinner table and probably more than you have seen in your life. Take a second and really imagine it...

Your spouse in craving a certain kind of fish they had visiting this town with their parents in childhood. You want to surprise them with the perfect fish dinner but you know nothing about fish. As you are walking through the overcrowded market you hear the fisherman yelling their fares and calling the crowd to their booths. This is fascinating to you as you have never seen anything like it coming from the corner grocery store in the suburbs. One fisherman in particular stands out to you, a master orator (he has probably been at this since his own childhood). He calls to the crowd, selling his fish with flash and class, clearly a master of the craft. As you're watching this gifted salesman and the mass of people gathering around him you suddenly become overwhelmed. The hype of the moment has passed and reality sinks in that the evening is soon approaching and you are no closer to your goal now than you were an hour ago. When a sense of failure start to set in , you suddenly feel a tap on your shoulder, and turning around you see a simple fisherman who inquires to what has brought you to the market today. The relief! The only person you have talked to all day and there aren't fifty people standing between the two of you! You engage in a lengthy conversation where this humble fisherman shows you a combination of care, interest, and a deep understanding of the fish your spouse is looking for. You became so enthralled with the conversation that you lose track of time and realize you need to be heading home, fish in hand of course. You resolve to go back to the same market the next day to stop by the humble stand and report back on the success you had using his tips! You have more questions about the assortment of fish available in this unique part of the world. There are still countless stands but something is different the second day.

So the question that needs to be asked is this: Who are you going to go to with your questions?

Odds are you will go back to ask the fisherman who you had the chance to get to know one on one. Why is that? The other fisherman seemed to know just as much (or at least be able to tell you as much in a just as interesting manner), and all the other shoppers at the market seemed to be quite taken with the first fisherman and many of the other loud fisherman for that matter. However, you had the chance to sit with the humble fisherman, get to know him one on one, and that person proved to you that they not only know a lot about fish, but that they have a genuine interest in your well-being. And he was "just" a fisherman for goodness' sakes.

Now you may be asking yourself, what does fish or fisherman have anything to do with leadership? Well, more than you'd think in this case. Theodore Roosevelt, the 26th president of the United States, is quoted as first voicing the popular line, "People don't care how much you know, until they know how much you care". In our guided scenario, the humble fisherman has demonstrated a leadership quality that cannot be ignored, and most certainly should be learned by any leader endeavoring to be impactful. The quality can be summed up in a few words: compassion, caring, genuineness, investment, and authenticity. The humble fisherman illustrated most perfectly what President Roosevelt was trying to teach, and what the first fisherman lacked. The first fisherman surely knew his craft, and obviously was a great orator and extremely charismatic. However, the first fisherman was not INVESTED in the people who were buying his fish. The first fisherman's investment was appealing to the buyers so that he would make as much money as possible selling his fish. The humble fisherman, however, took the time to visit with his buyer and teach them what he knew about fish, not just the superficial facts that would get the buyer to purchase his product. The humble fisherman's investment was in the ONE, in that person's betterment and real needs.

When you think of a leader who excels in one on one leadership, what words come to your mind? Perhaps you think of the word mentor? Or possibly a guide? Maybe you are thinking of an individual in particular, that coach you took a personal interest in your success, or a teacher who gave you that extra tutoring session during their lunch hour to make sure you understood the curriculum. Maybe it's the principal who called you into their office because they knew you were going through a hard time at home, or a guidance counselor who researched possible career fields on their own time after a perplexing aptitude test? All of these people and more are demonstrating what one on one leadership is all about, and that's the ONE, being you. Your knowledge, your future, your success, your progress, your well-being.

The Allazo Group

In closing, think about the leader that you would like to be. Would you like to be the leader that demonstrates their flashy knowledge to the masses, demonstrating your charisma to be recognized by the crowds? Or would you like to be the leader that takes the time to invest in the one, knowing that the greatest joy in leadership comes from seeing the success of others around you? I will give you space in a few words to answer that question, but there is one more fact to the story that you might find interesting. The first fisherman had to hustle every day to sell a few fish because eventually his flash wore off to most and new customers had to be reeled in daily, just like his product. The humble fisherman made more money because he has repeat customers who refused to go anywhere but his stand because of the impact he had made not only on their dinner table but their lives. Remember President Roosevelt's words when these decisions have to be made: People don't care how much you know, until they know how much you care."

_____

_____

_____

_____

_____

_____

_____

_____

_____

_____

_____

_____

_____

Coaching

The story above is effective in relaying the power of taking personal interest. Coaching is the tool a leader uses to make that personal attention empowering and beneficial to not only the individual but the organization.

When we think of coaching we might think of a PE coach from the 9th grade with whistle in hand and gym shorts to boot. All joking aside, sport's coaches can and should have a powerful influence on those student athletes with whom they interact. But coaching in an organizational setting is different, it has a different skill set that needs to be mastered and a different value that it brings to an organization. Coaching in sports involves a lot of yelling out directions and may contain a real need for short term motivations. Coaching in business, government or education is about empowering others through guiding them to their own answers, their own capabilities and their own values.

Entire books have been written on Coaching and we offer workshops through The Allazo Group on the subject. But if you really want to understand empowerment as a leader, you HAVE to understand the fundamentals and principles of coaching. We want to address some key principles here. We call the following:

A Crash Course in Coaching

- It is an honor to be trusted as a coach, treat it that way. Do your best to be unbiased while still being intensely focused on the individual. Clear all distractions when you take on a coaching role and help the coachee feel like an equal.

- Never put yourself in an inappropriate situation, make sure all encounters are HR certified. That may not be as intense as it sounds, but it is good to cover all of your bases.

- You are not a dispensary of information or the source of all knowledge, you will be at your best if you realize you are a guide.

- You have to listen and listen the right way, too often we think we are listening but are only listening partially or in a less effective way. Consider the following:

As written by Maria Konnikova, "Indeed, so poorly are we at actually taking someone else's point of view that when we are explicitly requested to do so, we still proceed from an egocentric place. In one series of studies, researchers found that people adopt the perspective of others by simply from their own. It's a question of degree rather than type: We tend to begin with our own view as an anchoring point, and then adjust slightly in one direction instead of altering the view altogether. Moreover, once we reach an estimate that sounds satisfactory to us,we stop thinking and consider the problem resolved. We've successfully captured the required point of view. That tendency is known as satisficing, a blend of sufficing and satisfying: a response error that errs on the egocentric side of plausible answers to a given question. As soon as we find an answer that satisfies, we stop looking, whether or not the answer is ideal or even remotely accurate. (In a recent study on online behavior, for instance, individuals were profoundly influenced by existing personal preferences in their evaluations of websites-- and they used those preferences for an anchor to reduce the number of sites they considered and to terminate their online search. As a result, they returned often to already known sites, instead of taking the time to evaluate potential new sources of information, and they chose to focus on search engine summaries as opposed to actual site visits to make their decisions.) The tendency towards an egocentric bias in satisfying is especially strong when a plausible answer is presented early on in the search process. We then tend to complete our task complete, even if it's far from being so."

5. Ask effective questions that help people to explore their desires, their motivations and skills. Examples of effective questions include:

- Why do YOU think your department is underperforming?
- Why do YOU think your department is achieving such effective roles?
- What would you like to accomplish from this time together?
- What resources do you need to be successful? Why?
- Why needs to be involved in this conversation to really achieve our purpose?
- What is one thing you can do this week to improve on what you have talked about? Will you come back at this time next week and report back to me?

6. Developing skills is always better than developing dependency on others. The purpose of coaching is to create other leaders.

7. Coaching is about fostering improvement through guidance but not about asserting your will. Asserting your will usually comes in lecture form and lecturing is not coaching.

8. Remember that accountability is key. Give an assignment and expect your coachee to follow up. If they do not follow up or keep their commitments, there is no need to be rude but you must explain there is no reason to move forward with your coaching sessions until the coachee fulfills their commitment. Lesson B comes after Lesson A, and it's the coachee that dictates the lessons learned.

Provide People Opportunities to Grow

Are we disciplined enough to help others to constantly improve as we ourselves constantly improve? It is one thing to help yourself and a whole other level of talent to constantly create an environment where others around you can improve. With discipline and planning, it can be done. The reality is… it must be done. So, what can we do as leaders to provide opportunities for improvement?

- Create both structured and unstructured learning environments. Encourage people to attend seminars, download podcasts and read diligently. At the same time, create structured environments where your people can meet in small groups, discuss issues, find solutions and gain new perspectives. Set up large group meetings where senior leaders are able to share their insights and lessons from their career.

- When you feel people are becoming complacent in their assignments or have mastered what has been asked of them, be quick to give praise and invite them to newer and broader assignments.
- If possible, create a formal mentorship program within your organization using the guidelines from earlier in the book. Senior leaders who would never before be interacting with junior members of the organization will provide fresh perspectives and growth for both groups.

With this commitment to growth in mind, consider the words of Benjamin Franklin, "Without continual growth and progress, such words as **improvement**, **achievement** and **success** have no meaning." It's our opinion that this quote should be looked at as more of a flow chart than as a statement.

When broken down in that simple flow chart, it makes every growth opportunity measurable. Is there improvement? Is it leading to higher achievement? If no, something needs to change, if yes, we have success.

So in summary: A true leader must be able to cultivate improvement in their organization on a daily basis. If improvement can be reached, then the improved individual must be led to additional achievements that will finally create success. Success cannot be so far out of reach that is seems unobtainable. It must be palatable. It must be broken down into steps.

For example, we have a close friend who is currently training for an Ironman triathlon. An Ironman consists of a 2.4-mile swim, 112-mile bike race, and a full 26.2-mile marathon. All this must be done in the specified amount of time. At first glance, the success of becoming an Ironman seems incredibly unachievable. Who in their right mind would try something like this? Is it even possible? It might seem impossible without seeing small and consistent improvements every day. Reaching a daily and a weekly and a monthly achievement is improvement and is eventually going to lead the individual down the path of a successful finish to their race.

Whether in a seemingly impossible test of physical strength or in a seemingly impossible test of organizational growth, remember the formula.

Empowering is a Cycle

As said, empowering is not a one-time event, it is a cycle in and of itself. In fact, there are several levels of empowerment cycles resulting from how you are empowered by your own actions, empowered by your peers and those you trust in your inner circle, and, finally, by your leaders. You not only receive the benefit of these cycles, but you also have the opportunity to be the facilitators of these cycles in the different roles you play.

Empowered by Yourself Might Look Something Like This

Self-Direction comes from an understanding your purpose and your role in the organization

    This leads to action, results and then natural Self Evaluation

        From Self Evaluation comes a clearer understanding and Self Correction

            When Self Correction takes its course and improvement comes to fruition this naturally leads to

                Self Confidence.

When Self Confidence is established and used to do more and be more, you will come back to a higher level of Self Direction and thus the cycle of Self-Empowerment begins again!

Empowered by Peers

Those in your inner circle will likely be those who stand by you and empower you in your everyday opportunities and challenges. The empowerment cycle that a friend or peer can invite can take countless forms, but one might look like this: You have something you are trying to improve, often it will be respectfully pointed out by those around you.

Thus starts the cycle, Need for Improvement

⬇

leads to those around you encouraging you and empowering you to make

⬇

Small Victories, which consist not of self-mastery overnight but step by step improvement that over time leads to

⬇

Large Victories or a solution to the problem which leads

⬇

To a strong feeling of Empowerment based off evidence and not arrogance

⬇

Which will leave you humble enough to accept observations from your peers on something new you can improve on to be the best leader you can be and then

⬇

The process starts over.

Empowered by Leaders

Your Leader Coaches You and Helps You to Find Your Unique Talents and Resources You Bring to Your Organization

Guides you in how to use those gifts to the betterment of the organization

You implement those gifts over time and in the right settings with the guidance of your mentor

You see success and are empowered to do even more

The cycle begins again.

We all must learn to recognize these cycles and accept them as part of our journey in the Leadership Revolution. When we master these processes with humility and diligence, we have the advantage of so much more than our own point of view. These aren't just cycles we take advantage of at work, but cycles that we ought to take advantage of in every aspect of our lives. They are a key ingredient to the strength needed to ascend to highest levels of the Revolution.

UNITE

The Power of Uniting

The next step in our ascent upward in the leadership revolution is to unite your team. Becoming the leader, you need to be won't accomplish this, nor will empowering those around you. They are both essential steps in the unification process but are in no way the solution. The power to unite is a skill all its own and is crucial to the livelihood of your organization.

Uniting a team means more than just having everyone on the same page, it means having everyone believing the same things and working together to go the same place. To unite a team means everyone coming to have realistic expectations for other members of the team and communicating with you and others openly and often.

When a team unites, the chances for conflict decrease, the reality of productivity increases and the overall happiness of the organization is sustainable. This is power worth obtaining, power worth working for. It is power that has transformed organizations for generations. Let's take a look at a few examples from diverse industries:

- **The Golden State Warriors:** For years the Golden State Warriors struggled slightly tilting the scale toward mediocrity in the National Basketball Association, the world's premier basketball league. In 2015, they did the unthinkable, taking an unconventional roster and strategy, defeating the globe's best players in route to their first world championship in four decades. But how did the improbable materialize into a legendary championship run?

Much of the credit lies with the Warrior's first year head coach, Steve Kerr. A product of a brilliant upbringing and the tutelage of Hall of Fame coaches such as Lute Olson, Phil Jackson and Gregg Popovich, Kerr was well prepared for the challenge of uniting what he saw as a team with great potential. No doubt, most would think this unification process took place inside coach and player meetings in the locker room. Not so. It all started with a marketing meeting where executives throughout the 200 employee team met to discuss a marketing strategy.

Wanting to be inclusive they invited Kerr to the meeting to discuss the business side of the franchise. When asked his thoughts on any possible slogans, Kerr responded without any hesitation. "Strength in numbers." To him, winning a championship wasn't going to take the depth of the entire roster but the combined effort of every single member of the organization.

The marketing department ran with it and the entire organization, as well local fans rallied behind it. The results speak for themselves. Career starters took roles as reserves, coaches sacrificed on behalf of the team, fans poured in at record numbers and behind the scenes unity increased within the organization as a feeling something special was happening reached a climax. True to his word, Kerr did not forget those individuals who made up the numbers that gave him and his team strength. Before the unveiling of championship memorabilia, Kerr and his staff held a private party for the CEO all the way to the janitors of Oracle Arena to show they were just as much a part of the team as the players.

Often slogans are thrown around as nice ideas that may be remembered on occasion. True champions, and true leaders, live those slogans as they are embedded in their hearts. This basketball team serves as an example of unity that can be applied in any leadership capacity.

- **Abt Associates:** In Adam Bryant's brilliant New York Time's article from 2013, he discusses the power and challenges of unifying an organization. In one particular interview with Kathleen L. Flanagan, Chief Executive of Abt Associates, the world's first company to really master social accounting, he asks her about her experience in unifying a large and diverse organization.

She made the profound comment, "We've grown from $180 million in annual revenue a few years ago to $425 million today. As the company grew, more business units were created, and so we had more silos in the organization. My objective two years ago in coming into this job was to take down the silos. So I reorganized the company. It used to be organized around lines of business — international, U.S.-based, data collection — and there used to be senior vice presidents who led each of those big businesses. I took those senior V.P. positions away and hired one executive vice president for global business who shared my vision for what I call One Global Abt. At the heart of that is taking down the walls so people can collaborate more freely, so that we can leverage all of Abt. We now ask people to pick their heads up out of their project work or their division focus and look across the whole company. So I now ask my managers to wear two hats. Everybody's got their job in the big picture of the company, but they all have to wear an Abt hat. It's really easy, given the time pressures and the pace of our work, to put blinders on and be very project-focused. It's harder to take a step back and ask, "How does this apply to the whole company?"

What silos or cliques currently exist in your organization?

_____
_____
_____
_____
_____
_____

How do you think they were created?

_____
_____
_____
_____
_____

What are three things you can do today to begin tearing them down and instead build a unified culture?

1.

2.

3.

- **101st Airborne Division- The Band of Brothers:** The Band of Brothers, immortalized in by Executive Producers Steven Spielberg and Tom Hanks' HBO mini-series of the actual events a brave and dedicated brotherhood of young men faced in WWII, are perhaps the best known unit of

American soldiers to fight in the European front in the last centuries deadliest conflict. This group of young men known as "Easy Company" essentially battled their way from their initial parachute landings in the bomb filled night at Normandy all the way to Hitler's Eagle's nest with its haunted yet breath taking view.

To the members of Easy Company, much of the credit of the formation of one of the most unified teams in the history of the world came from the courageous yet humble example of Lieutenant Dick Richards, who selflessly sacrificed, mentored, fought and comforted his troops in the deadliest of firefights and the coldest of winter nights. In his published memoirs he talks about the leadership lessons he learned in the war. One powerful lessons he teaches on unifying comes in his view of his own leadership responsibilities. In essence, he explains that he would look himself in the mirror every night when possible and ask himself if he did his very best, for his men, his country and himself. This led to his attitude that it didn't matter who got credit but that the job was done and that a true leader will remain humble and EARN respect by being a leader of impeccable character.

Over the course of his career, historian Stephen E. Ambrose masterfully captures the essence of these young soldier's sacrifices for one another and the unique unity they formed in time of ultimate crisis where the fate of the free world hung in the balance. In his award winning book, he makes several insights, illustrating the power of unity, "Within Easy Company they had made the best friends they had ever had, or would ever have. They were prepared to die for each other; more important, they were prepared to kill for each other." Why? They rallied behind a cause and belief that they felt worth fighting and dying for. Much of this came from the consistent example of Commanding General of the Allied Forces, future President Dwight D. Eisenhower. "No matter how bad things got, no matter how anxious the staff became, the commander had to "preserve optimism in himself and in his command. Without confidence, enthusiasm and optimism in the command, victory is scarcely obtainable." Eisenhower realized that "optimism and pessimism are infectious and they spread more rapidly from the head downward than in any other direction." He learned that a commander's optimism "has a most extraordinary effect upon all with whom he comes in contact. With this clear realization, I firmly determined that my mannerisms and speech in public would always reflect the cheerful certainty of victory—that any pessimism and discouragement I might ever feel would be reserved for my pillow."

Ambrose sums up his thoughts as such, "At the core, the American citizen soldiers knew the difference between right and wrong, and they didn't want to live in a world in which wrong prevailed. So they fought, and won, and we all of us, living and yet to be born, must be forever profoundly grateful."

To unify a team much more needs to exist than the dynamic speeches of one charismatic leader. There needs to be vision grounded in something worth believing in, backed by leaders with the courage to do what it takes to sacrifice for the betterment of their team. Unity is the natural product of this kind of selfless leadership because at that point, everyone feels unquestionably unified in the sacred responsibility of leadership.

Sincerity and Empowerment

Oprah Winfrey has stated, "I've talked to nearly 30,000 people...they all wanted validation...They want to know; do you hear me? Do you see me? Does what I say mean anything to you?"

Elevating people around us gives life meaning for them and for us. Each of us is born with gifts to offer and for challenges we face every day. It is easy for us to elevate those people we like and also have easily recognizable gifts. We believe that is in some part because their gifts enrich our own lives. They serve us and we know if we acknowledge them, they will continue to empower US. But, what about the challenges we face in ourselves and in others? How do we elevate those individuals?

First, as talked about in Becoming, before we elevate anyone, we have to check in with ourselves. We need to determine if our intentions or motives are pure. We have all encountered the insincere compliment. Although it was nice to receive it, it was not fulfilling. We doubted its authenticity; the intentions of the compliment were given purely for the person giving it. We recommend a formula we try to apply around The Allazo Office. Before giving the compliment, ask yourself, can I give this compliment with sincerity? Do I really mean it? Does it come from my heart?

Recently, one of our own spoke with her former boss and thanked him for the sincerity of his compliments. In her words, "He pushed me, questioned me, moved me out of my comfort zone, challenged me, with my craft. When I received recognition from him for a job well done, I knew I earned it and deserved it. They were few and far between and sometimes years before I received them, but they were given with his complete knowledge and recognition that I had earned it. I felt the authenticity of the praise and it meant something to me and elevated my spirit."

One teacher we interviewed said, "The biggest challenge is recognizing and elevating the student whose challenges dominate his or her personality. I believe every person has her gifts and her challenges. When we are facing the challenges in the moment and on a constant basis, it is so difficult to remember the person's gifts. Often, the person identifies with his challenge because it has been his only recognition from others in life. I remind myself, as I often ponder a solution to discipline and education in the classroom, of the gift the student has to offer and how I can best facilitate it, recognize it, and begin to witness it daily."

Of those 30,000 people Oprah has talked with, they all, we all, seek for sincerity and recognition of who we are and what we have to offer the planet. Our sincerity must come from our hearts and for the purpose of uplifting those around us. If we fulfill acts of kindness or even do our daily job for our own purposes, we are not creating the world we think we are or need to. It is hollow and has little meaning. All our thoughts **must** come from a sincere heart. All our words **must** be spoken with sincere integrity. And then, and only then, all our actions will come from that sincere place of our soul and change lives and organizations.

Activity: Briefly list the people in your life who offer you challenges. If you wish, you may list the challenges you have with them. It is interesting, but you may discover that there is a theme that connects all these people. Consider that the challenges you face with them are their gift to you. The gift of allowing you to overcome the fear they represent.

_____

_____

_____

_____

_____

_____

_____

_____

_____

_____

Now, list the gifts these people have to offer, not only you, but those around them.

_____

_____

_____

_____

_____

_____

_____

_____

_____

_____

Contemplate strategies for acknowledging their gifts.

_____

_____

_____

_____

_____

_____

Consider how to implement your strategies and record your outcomes.

_____

_____

_____

_____

_____

_____

_____

_____

_____

_____

_____

_____

_____

_____

_____

_____

_____

_____

_____

The Allazo Group

Acknowledge the gifts and the outcomes to your challenge mentor.
Let him know how appreciative you are from a sincere heart.

Reflect on the outcome, once the process is complete reflect on
how you feel. Did it change the relationship? Did you change? If
not, repeat again trying another approach.

_____

_____

_____

_____

_____

_____

_____

_____

_____

_____

_____

_____

_____

_____

_____

_____

_____

_____

_____

_____

_____

_____

Example:

Egocentric Boss—Challenges: Selfish, always gives to receive something back, keeps score

Gifts: A great motivator, strategist and results oriented.

Strategies: Stop keeping score myself, ask for help in boss's strengths, keep my heart sincere with the gifts this boss has and not his challenges

Outcome: Great ideas for me to use in my own work life, tips I used in motivating in front of an audience

Reflect:

_____
_____
_____
_____
_____
_____
_____
_____
_____
_____
_____
_____
_____
_____

Keep in mind that life is for learning. We may take on the challenge, see amazing results, only to forget as everyday life continues around us. Several detours may occur, we forget what we did, and the relationship goes back to the way it was. It may not work, and we give up. The strategies quit working and so do we. These are not reasons to give up. They are opportunities to do a reality check with ourselves, get real with ourselves (Am I coming from a place of sincerity?), and start all over. Life is a cycle just like the Leadership Revolution, one challenge is successfully met and another presents itself, allowing us to grow in our wisdom and the use of the tools we have learned along the way.

Getting Buy in from Key Players

In striving to create a united organization, you need to first empower those who have the most influence over those around them. In this case, let's use a medium sized company for our case study.

The CEO has a great idea. In fact, it's an idea she thinks will change the entire fabric of the organization for good. The bottom line will go up, processes will become more streamlined and those are just a few of the many obvious benefits. The CEO has a close and even strong relationships with her vice presidents. They have followed her faithfully for years and their divisions have performed well. Turnover is almost unheard of.

The CEO plans and plans, every number, every detail. Finally, the time comes to unveil this new strategy. Sure it will mean mixing up some roles and changing a little of what happens from day to day, but it will work. It will work! The CEO calls a meeting filled with a catered lunch, seating charts, the whole nine yards. She stands up and lays out this new plan of action with detail, data and determination.

Fast forward 24 hours. The company is in chaos. Her VP's are overran by the complaints they are receiving from employees from across the company. There are threats to quit, VP's that feel betrayed and no excitement for the plan, to say the least. What could have possibly gone wrong?

In your mind, reading the story above, what was wrong in the CEO's strategy?

_____

_____

_____

_____

_____

_____

_____

_____

_____

_____

_____

_____

_____

_____

_____

_____

Well, the real key to the whole situation is that she didn't get buy in from those with the most influence in her organization. They were blindsided and never had the opportunity to take in the plan and see the benefits for themselves. Forced to make a decision on the spot, many panicked. When hit with hard questions, they were left without adequate information despite the PowerPoint (of which they had no copy).

So if you were to tell the exact same story a second time in an idealistic way, how would it be different?

_____

_____

_____

_____

_____

_____

_____

_____

_____

_____

_____

_____

_____

_____

_____

_____

_____

Something like this would likely have more success:

The CEO has a great idea. In fact, it's an idea she thinks will change the entire fabric of the organization for good. The bottom line will go up, processes will become more streamlined and those are just a few of the many obvious benefits. The CEO has a close and even strong relationships with her vice presidents. They have followed her faithfully for years and their divisions have performed well. Turnover is almost unheard of. That is why the very first thing she does is calls in her second in command and runs her plan by him. They hammer out some potential problems that may come up if presented to the organization as a whole. They also talk about the Vice Presidents and departments that will be most effective. The next day they schedule meetings with each vice president and solicit their advice. Some very practical changes are made as they help each VP see how their role will shape the future of the organization. At the end of the day all the Vice Presidents meet with the CEO and her second in command to go over details of the plan, and answer questions that might be posed over the next few days. The Vice Presidents take the night to sleep on it and they meet again the next morning, repeating the process. In the end there is buy in and excitement.

After the executive team plans every detail and how it will affect each department the time finally comes to unveil this new strategy. Instead of a large meeting, each VP takes the plan and the parts specific to their department and meet with their department directors who in turn meet with the individuals of the department. The CEO does her best to be at every meeting to answer questions, the VP's are also well equipped to answer questions. Finally, a large group meeting is held and it is more of a workshop than an unveiling. The CEO answers questions from the audience, reiterates her excitement and breaks the audience into small departmental groups to plan and strategize. Everyone feels a part of the plan. Everyone takes ownership.

Comparing the two stories, what factors need to be in place to make the second story possible?

_____

_____

_____

_____

_____

_____

_____

_____

_____

_____

_____

_____

_____

_____

_____

_____

_____

Team Values

Coming back to Team Values from a unifying perspective, consider this conundrum many organizations find themselves in and contemplate possible solutions that fit your organization.

We recently interviewed one of the up and coming stars of his state's business scene, we met in his office out west and chatted for about an hour. On the wall just outside his window were the corporate values his team embraced. We asked him about those values and how they related to unity. He said, "They aren't just random words we put together. They are meant to complement each other, to build the individual while building the team. They align with our mission perfectly." One of us asked, "Is that a hard thing to strive for?" He responded emphatically, "Striving to be doesn't work. They have...to...be...REAL core values. These are the skills and behaviors that matter most, there is no striving." What he was teaching us was that things like integrity, accountability, diligence, those aren't things you strive for, those are baseline values you build on. He went on to say, "Our employees know it is by those values their performance is measured, their advancement is determined and at the same time the way we help our employees create paths to improvement." He taught us that in his experience, it doesn't matter how much you understand about teams if your own team doesn't have core values they believe in and abide by.

With that said, consider your organization's core values. Fill in the blanks with those values and spend a day observing your organization. Circle on the scale how realistically your organization embraces those values with a 1 being they don't even know it exists and a 10 being it is in the heart of every employee.

_____   1 - 2 - 3 - 4 - 5 - 6 - 7 - 8 - 9 - 10

_____   1 - 2 - 3 - 4 - 5 - 6 - 7 - 8 - 9 - 10

_____   1 - 2 - 3 - 4 - 5 - 6 - 7 - 8 - 9 - 10

_____   1 - 2 - 3 - 4 - 5 - 6 - 7 - 8 - 9 - 10

_____   1 - 2 - 3 - 4 - 5 - 6 - 7 - 8 - 9 - 10

_____   1 - 2 - 3 - 4 - 5 - 6 - 7 - 8 - 9 - 10

What needs to change in your organization to make your values more realistic? What values need to be added or modified?

_____

_____

_____

_____

_____

How can you create a culture of unity and accountability behind your team's values?

_____

_____

_____

_____

_____

_____

_____

_____

_____

_____

How Teams Work

Teams are complex. Be it figuratively, they are in essence, living, breathing organisms with a heart and a soul. Though it is not figurative in the slightest to say that the individuals who make up an organization possess hearts, souls, desires, ambitions, habits and personalities. To treat a team as a machine is a calamity of catastrophic proportions. To understand how to best unite your team, you'll need to understand how teams work.

The presence or the absence of unity depends largely on the decisions, assignments, modeling and culture established by senior leaders. Teamwork, at its core, is collaboration. But collaboration can be forced upon a team about as effectively as one can walk and hold water with cusped hands. It may appear possible at a glance, but time will prove its inevitable failure.

In the words of Wal-Mart's founder Sam Walton, "We're all working together, that's the secret." From his perspective that obviously was the secret to Wal-Mart's rise to a global brand and household name. However, if Mr. Walton were here with you today as you read this book, the real secret you should inquire about is HOW those early Walmart employees came to work together.

So the real question is, is it possible to understand how teams work? Yes, but thousands of institutions across the world are still being funded to explore the concept. As long as the human mind continues to be as vast and complex as the very galaxy we live in, there will always be infinitely more to both learn and apply. With that said, there are some timeless principles every person in the Revolution of effective leadership should know and can begin to apply today. Let's explore a few.

- **Teams thrive in a team first environment**: It sounds obvious, but billions of dollars are wasted each year by managers wishing to create a more unified team. It's not that it's impossible to create a unified team, it's just that there is usually something deeper in play than just changing how people act, it's the very culture of the organization that is poisoning the possibility of a real team atmosphere.

This concept is powerfully taught by one of the world's foremost and respected thought leaders on teams and organizations, Mr. Simon Sinek. In a revolutionary talk and in lectures repeatedly given around the world, Sinek speaks about how great leaders build thriving teamwork environments. "In the military, they give medals for people who are willing to sacrifice themselves so that others may survive. In business, we give bonuses to people who sacrifice others." We all know there is something wrong with this picture. Sadly, it is the culture in most organizations throughout the world. But no one ever said it HAD to be that way. Again, quoting Sinek, "Great leaders are willing to sacrifice the numbers to save the people. Poor leaders sacrifice the people to save the numbers. When a family makes less money, they don't get rid of one of their children. They go from name brand Cheerios to generic Cheerios. Same idea: Make everyone a part of it and say, "Okay, guys we don't want to have layoffs so we all need to work together to find efficiencies."

People feel safe when their leaders sacrifice for them as opposed to always being asked to sacrifice for their leader. A young man we know intimately was once under the tutelage of a leader at the Virginia Military Institute and witnessed him give numerous trainings. He noticed his mentor always waiting to get in line for dinner until after everyone else was through and seated. In asking this veteran leader why he did this, even though he had been the one speaking as the leader of the group, he simply said, "We must always remember, officers eat last." In contemplating that lesson, the young man realized the powerful principle of sacrificing for the team and the message it sent to those from all over the globe looking towards this prestigious leader as an example. No doubt this lesson without words is now impacting teams throughout the world.

There is only "WE": Them vs. Us, My guys vs. Your Guys, that "other" building, the big shots upstairs. Have you ever heard a variation of one of these? We're sure you have. We all have.

Division is a dangerous notion. No one said healthy competition was a bad thing, but if it is the lifeblood your organization depends on for survival, your organization simply won't survive. One of the hardest things a leader is asked to do is to create a culture of "We" and root out the two separate cultures of "We and They". We know efforts to unite are successful, as was the case with Abt. Yet there are some practical reasons teams struggle to unite.

1. Just because people are put into teams does not mean they will act as a team. A team is only as good as the level that people accept their team environment. If there is a feeling of force or ulterior motives, it doesn't matter if a group of people look like a team, they won't function as a team.

2. Teams often aren't adequately prepared to be a team. There is an old saying that was once shared with us, "If you get enough ~~men~~ people around the hood of the car staring at the engine, you may not solve the problem but you will look like you're getting there." It's the same with teams at work, school or anywhere else. Bodies do not equal strategical brain power.

3. By committing to the team concept you are inevitably diverting time, a highly profitable resource, away from the natural course a talented individual would take in problem solving. This time is now spent team building, trust exercises and getting to know each other's "styles". This isn't necessarily a bad thing in the long run, but an obstacle none the less.

With that said, there are some strategies that help promote the "We" mentality and break down these barriers. Employed in the highest levels of the revolution and backed in data, they are proven to be most likely to succeed if viewed and applied in the right context.

- **Be Deliberate:** We know throwing together a group of people and telling them to unite is not an effective way to form a team. Teamwork isn't a catchphrase, it takes deliberate and thought out planning. Examples of questions you might ask yourself as the leader are: Who should be on the team and why? In what atmosphere would this group of people most likely succeed? What conflicts will arise with this group of personalities and how can we proactively resolve them? Who should be in what role and why? How can I help everyone on the tem to feel valued? Being deliberate will protect some of your most precious assets, including human capital, trust, money, innovation and time.

- **Determine Decision Making Procedures:** Establish clear procedures in regards to decision making within the team. This will not only reduce friction but increase efficiency when expectations and processes are clearly in place. The first step, obviously is to determine the question the team needs to answer or the problem than needs to be solved. From there some things to consider include; ways in which evidences are presented, who had the ultimate say per the established roles, whether decisions need to be unanimous or if possible solutions are going to be brought to senior leaders. Knowing the answers to these questions will disintegrate the conflict so many teams meet when trying to come to consensus.

Along with removing the negative aspects of decision making it also brings added benefits. Having decision making procedures in place will ensure that everyone is thinking about the same things while retaining their unique perspectives. (You never want to stifle innovation or individual thought!) They will also be engaged on the same topics at the same time all while keeping talking points on the same level and pointed towards the targeted goal. Those same decision making procedures should also include provisions for equal input, invaluable within itself in creating a "WE" culture.

- **Provide Safety in the Mission:** Many people fear that teams will ultimately outshine the individual work and skills they bring to their organization. More than just a fear of not receiving due credit, there is often a fear of losing their job. Here is one example of an interview we had with a teacher in the United States, "I was assigned to work in a team with a number of my coworkers, a few of them really negative and outspoken. They naturally became the leaders of the group as they were the leaders of the clique's within the faculty. Our principal had been laying people off who weren't up to par and I had always been given outstanding reviews on my teaching and professionalism. Whether irrational or not, I began to fear if these negative leaders of our "team" were the ones in the principal's ear, that it could tarnish my impeccable reputation I had built over decades and maybe even lead to me losing my job. I dreaded every day assigned as a teamwork day. I felt there was no team, just a show to advance someone else's career by throwing their "team" under the bus." Powerful words that are not uncommon in our interactions with members of the most diverse of organizations.

People perform best when they feel safe. The old acronym for TEAM actually works here, Together Everyone Achieves More. So here's the question, does everyone feel safe enough to where there is an actual environment where everyone achieves more? When people are united in their mission and feel safe to express themselves and work together without any worry of repercussion, the "WE" mentality can grow and thrive.

So knowing something of team dynamics, honestly answer the following questions to analyze the team mentality in your own organization!

What kind of sacrifices do leaders in your organization make most often (People, Numbers, Reputations, etc.)?

_____

_____

_____

_____

_____

_____

How united is your team behind a common cause?

_____

_____

_____

_____

_____

_____

The Allazo Group

What can you change to help people feel more safe in your organization?

_____

_____

_____

_____

_____

_____

What can you do today, this week, this month and this year to create a stronger "WE" culture?

_____

_____

_____

_____

_____

_____

_____

_____

_____

_____

_____

_____

_____

In your efforts to form sustainable teams, remember the words of Henry Ford, "Coming together is a beginning; keeping together is progress; working together is success." At the same time, find inspiration in the words of Helen Keller, who herself naturally knew more about teams than just about any CEO. "Alone we can do so little. Together we can do so much." Your efforts to build safe, sustainable and vision filled teams is crucial in the ascension of the leadership revolution.

Red Flags of Dysfunctionality

Many leaders don't see the walls of their organization crumbling around them due to the corrosion of disunity until they are sitting in the ruble asking themselves, "What happened?" Luckily, the wise leader sees the signs of dysfunctionality before they take root in their organization. There are red flags every leader should be aware of and nip in the bud the second they begin to sprout.

You know your team is dysfunctional if....

- Politics seem to be taking precedence over purpose.
- If results no longer matter to team members.
- If there is an abundance of blame and a clear absence of accountability.
- If people are disinterested in innovation and new horizons, viewing their role as simply fulfilling a job.
- If there is a distinct lack of trust in one another and senior leadership.
- If unethical, questionable or even illegal behavior are in any way justified.
- If there is a presence of cliques within the organization.
- If there is more backbiting than building one another.
- If you are spending more time dealing with conflict than you are coaching and building.

- If your turnover rate is higher than your retention.

Which of these, if any, have you seen in your organization? What are three strategies you can begin to implement to dissolve this disease known as dysfunctionality?

-
-
-

One Moral Flaw Ruins It All

With all this important exploration into the topic of unifying an organization, it is important to note that it takes time build lasting unity. It does not, however, take much time at all to ruin the unity you and your team worked so hard to build.

If trust is a key factor in building unity, then any act of a leader that diminishes trust will destroy that unity. The best way to destroy that trust is to live without integrity and make unethical decisions. Plain and simple. It sounds like such an easy thing to do, yet there are countless men and women who have forgotten or ignored this valuable idea that honesty is the best policy. Recent history has shown multitudes of once entrusted leaders that have not only found themselves out of favor with their organizations but in a prison cell as a result of unethical behavior.

But why? Why would someone risk their family, livelihood, reputation and future for acts of unethical behavior. Hopefully you will never know! Steve Tobak writing for CBS News in his June 2010 article gives some insights into possible reasons why some high powered CEOs make extremely unethical decisions. Though he is discussing CEO's of large companies, these same characteristics and habits can slip into the lives and justifications of any leader at any level and at any age. To know what to look out for in yourself and others is a key step in preventing the fatal fall off the leadership revolution.

Tobak's Hypothesis: What Motivates Rich, Powerful CEOs to Commit Fraud?

- **Greed.** Corporate America is often characterized as the land of greed; why shouldn't the folks at the top be the greediest of all? Actually, these CEOs risked way more wealth than they stood to gain by their fraudulent actions. I don't think any amount of money or power would have fulfilled the needs that made them commit these acts.

- **Arrogance.** Sam Waksal of ImClone described himself as arrogant in an interview after his conviction. Perhaps all that power and money makes CEOs feel invincible, untouchable, above the law. And maybe they got caught because, on some level, they knew what they were doing was wrong and wanted to be punished for it. Hmm.

- **Evil.** Well, evil is sort of a philosophical concept. In this context, perhaps it describes the effect the CEO's actions had on shareholders and employees, but I don't think it actually describes their behavior. I mean, they didn't torture little puppies or murder anybody.

- **Stupidity.** Maybe they're just plain stupid. No, I don't think so. Most of these people didn't just fall off the turnip truck. Look at Computer Associates, Enron, ImClone, Qwest, Tyco, WorldCom. These CEOs built huge, successful companies. I don't buy that any of them were anything but brilliant businessmen.

- **Personality Disorder.** Delusional, narcissistic psychopaths, call them what you want, it sounds like a no-brainer to me. I mean, most of these folks maintained their innocence to the end. That implies compartmentalization so they didn't actually feel empathy for those affected by their actions. Denial is a powerful thing. Sure sounds like a behavioral disorder to me. Anyway, there's no denying that each of these men functioned, and functioned exceptionally, until their issues caught up with them.

And that may be the lesson we can take away from Tobak's theory. Lies and deception will, in one way or another, always catch up to you. The journey of life's decisions starts with a first step. We would all be wise to be careful where we step.

Marie J. Kane, a veteran entrepreneur has taken it upon herself to interview company leaders across the country. One interview from a regular leader at a regular company in the American South truly illustrates what it means to "get it" in regards to integrity. "Integrity is incredibly important and it should be in your spine. You must make sure that you don't have two sets of values, one for yourself and one for your employees. When you have new people coming into the organization you have to let them know what the values are and make sure they understand. Then the leader has to be a living example. I think that the temptation is there once you are the leader to think that you can do as you please and that no one will notice or object. I think too that there is a lot of talk about being ethical and honest and treating employees and customers right and standing behind the product, but a lot of times companies set a price tag on what's right and wrong. If there is a problem then no matter what the cost is of fixing it, you have to do it. You've got to decide what your values are and then you have to follow them. Leading by example is the most important thing. You can't teach one way and do something else."

It may not be eloquent and it may not be from a fortune 500 CEO, but it rings true and is true. With this kind of attitude toward yourself first and those within your influence, lies the greatest chance of a united culture of integrity. Above all else you cannot set a price tag on right and wrong.

Consider this: Answer honestly, would your integrity be any different if the price at stake increased from 10 cents to 10 dollars, from 10 dollars to 10,000 dollars from 10,000 dollars to 10 million dollars? What is the worth of your integrity?

_____

_____

_____

_____

_____

_____

_____

_____

_____

Hallmarks of United Teams

Just as there are certain signs that are associated with dysfunctional teams, there are just as many positive signs you can easily recognize and associate with united teams. Unity is built and maintained over time. There is no one key ingredient to a united team but there are some strong indicators we have found over the years.

You know your team is united if:

- You see teamwork building trust, trust building people and people building a strong culture of excellence.
- Team members take responsibility for their own actions with a resolve to do better and be better and are met with support over resentment.
- Collaboration is the normal.
- People are too busy working for a common purpose that they don't have time to criticize others.
- There are open and productive conversations about performance issues that lead to real change and real growth.
- If an unbiased person walked into your office and asked, is this a "We" organization or a "Me" organization, just about everyone would say a "We" organization.
- Turnover is low, morale is high.
- People work together because they want to, not because they have to.

What are you striving for? We love the words of Vince Lombardi, "Individual commitment to a group effort- that is what makes a team work, a company work, a society work a civilization work." What is the denominator? One has to choose to be united to not only a cause but with the people behind the cause, only then is unity in an organization a reality.

Live Your Truth at ALL Times - Encourage Others to Do the Same

A wise mother once told her children that, "No matter what happens, what is falsely said about you, no matter what the circumstances you find in your life, ALWAYS LIVE YOUR TRUTH. Time will always bring the truth to light in regards to integrity. Your reputation may be taken from you with a single rumor, but your integrity is completely within your own control." In the powerful, timeless words of William Ernest Henley poem, "Invictus":

"Out of the night that covers me,
Black as the Pit from pole to pole,
I thank whatever gods may be
For my unconquerable soul.

In the fell clutch of circumstance
I have not winced nor cried aloud.
Under the bludgeonings of chance
My head is bloody, but unbowed.

Beyond this place of wrath and tears
Looms but the Horror of the shade,
And yet the menace of the years
Finds, and shall find, me unafraid.

It matters not how strait the gate,

How charged with punishments the scroll,
I am the master of my fate:
I am the captain of my soul."

Read the poem again... Let its words sink into your consciousness. Do you believe him? Does it start with you? Are you really in charge of your own future, your own integrity?

Integrity is a must not only for success as a leader but success in your personal life, family and all things that truly bring joy and fulfillment to one's existence. We would recommend the book, *How Will You Measure Your Life* by Harvard business professor, Clayton L. Christensen, to anyone wishing to obtain a personal conviction of their life's purpose. Based on a speech given at the Harvard Business School commencement ceremony in the Spring of 2010., Christensen explores a number of topics beneficial to the human family, in business and in life. One topic of particular appropriateness for this section is that of living your truth at all times. Christensen, in a Harvard Business School article, shares this insight in an excerpt from his book. We would all be wise to learn from it.

"Many of us have convinced ourselves that we are able to break our own personal rules "just this once." In our minds, we can justify these small choices. None of those things, when they first happen, feels like a life-changing decision. The marginal costs are almost always low. But each of those decisions can roll up into a much bigger picture, turning you into the kind of person you never wanted to be.

I came to understand the potential damage of "just this once" in my own life when I was in England, playing on my university's varsity basketball team. It was a fantastic experience; I became close friends with everyone on the team. We killed ourselves all season, and our hard work paid off-we made it all the way to the finals of the big tournament. But then I learned that the championship game was scheduled to be played on a Sunday. This was a problem. At age sixteen, I had made a personal commitment to God that I would never play ball on Sunday because it is our Sabbath.

So I went to the coach before the tournament finals and explained my situation. He was incredulous. "I don't know what you believe," he said to me, "but I believe that God will understand." Every one of the guys on the team came to me and said, "You've got to play. Can't you break the rule, just this one time?"

It was a difficult decision to make. The team would suffer without me. The guys on the team were my best friends. We'd been dreaming about this all year. I'm a deeply religious man, so I went away to pray about what I should do. As I knelt to pray, I got a very clear feeling that I needed to keep my commitment. So I told the coach that I wasn't able to play in the championship game.

In so many ways, that was a small decision—involving one of several thousand Sundays in my life. In theory, surely I could have crossed over the line just that one time and then not done it again. But looking back on it, I realize that resisting the temptation of "in this one extenuating circumstance, just this once, it's okay" has proved to be one of the most important decisions of my life. Why? Because life is just one unending stream of extenuating circumstances. Had I crossed the line that one time, I would have done it over and over and over in the years that followed.

And it turned out that my teammates didn't need me. They won the game anyway.

If you give in to "just this once," based on a marginal-cost analysis, you'll regret where you end up. That's the lesson I learned: it's easier to hold to your principles 100 percent of the time than it is to hold to them 98 percent of the time. The boundary—your personal moral line—is powerful because you don't cross it; if you have justified doing it once, there's nothing to stop you doing it again.

Decide what you stand for. And then stand for it all the time."

The reason the Allazo Group talks so often about little decisions is because if ignored, those decisions decide the destiny of your life. The best way to stay on course is to do everything in your power to not get off course. When we focus on the small things, the big things tend to take care of themselves.

What will you stand for? By making the decision today of what you will do and not do, no matter what the circumstance, you have no reason to make a decision concerning the temptations of tomorrow.

We are sure something came to mind in way of exceptions to your own rules or justifications to your own conscience. With that said, changing now, what WILL you stand for? You can refer back to your I Will Never and I Will Always document for inspiration.

_____

_____

_____

_____

_____

_____

_____

Nurturing Unity

We know that the entire purpose of the Leadership Revolution is to free up your days, to free up your thoughts and to free up your organizational culture to focus in a more laser like way on a common vision. You SHOULD NOT be the only one practicing this art in your organization. It needs to be practiced throughout your company, school, hospital or whatever organization you find yourself in. It should be practiced not only by individuals but by small groups of teams, departments and on an all-encompassing level.

Time, energy and resources are easily unaccounted for in the wasted minutes of an undisciplined organization. At the same time, if those you lead and those that lead others feel you are constantly putting out fires, they will never be free to really unite and reach their full potential. People, just as much as organizations, were never meant to constantly live in panic mode.

Freeing up time to build unity is essential. Desires are worthless without time to execute those desires through sincere actions. Once we have the time, what ways can we foster and nurture a unified organization? Here are ten ideas to get you started. Circle the yes or no after each description to see a clearer picture of your unifying efforts.

Recognize that every person in your organization has the capacity to be a leader one way or another. The best organizations we know are the ones who are willing to invest not just in their top level talent, but their rising level talent all the way down (or realistically, if they're doing it right, up) to their staff workers. Everyone has something to contribute through diverse experience and knowledge. When people are treated as leaders, even over their seemingly small stewardship, they tend to rise to the occasion. If you as a leader, recognize other leaders for their unique contributions to the mission of the organization, you will only strengthen commitment around that essential rallying point.

Do I treat EVERY member of the organization as leaders, even if they only lead themselves?

YES | NO

Refer often, even obsessively to your organizational purpose to keep your united front strong and growing. Nothing extinguishes the enthusiasm of a true and lasting purpose like ignoring it and those around you until someone with a higher rank than yours visits the office.

Additionally, every meeting, every holiday party, every formal conversation and even most of your informal conversations should reference the organization's purpose. It's not a practice as much as it becomes a way of life for the organizations doing it right. If done in the right spirit this commitment to a higher purpose becomes contagious. However, as you well know, this kind of commitment to an organizational purpose can only come when people feel safe and trust within the organization. It comes back to that oxygen mask speech at the beginning of every flight. You can't help others secure their gas mask until yours is fully on and receiving oxygen.

Do I refer to our purpose multiple times a day?

YES | NO

Help everyone in your entire organization to see and feel the vision and mission of the organization and the key role they play. No one should go a day in your organization without knowing the purpose of the organization and understanding how their work, no matter how small, fits into that masterful plan.

Have I had a talk with EVERY member of our organization about the critical role they play?

YES | NO

Preach the idea of WE, or FAMILY, or TEAM and as the leader, back it up in every one of your actions.

Do my actions promote a WE mentality within the organization?

YES | NO

Hire for Unity.

Do I look for candidates or potential members that fit into our unified team?

YES | NO

Don't coerce, build.

Do I build others around me at every opportunity?

YES | NO

Set the example, servant leadership.

Am I an example of the kind of leadership I want within my organization?

YES | NO

Acknowledge wins.

Do I acknowledge far more wins than I do failures?

YES | NO

Give people a reason to care.

Is there evidence that our organization's members or that I care about more than just a paycheck?

YES | NO

Have a realistic view:

Does my story of the organization's culture about the same as the stories told by other members of the organization?

YES | NO

Help the Whole Team to See

None of these important principles of nurturing and building unity should be ignored, but if we had to pick one to emphasize right here, right now as you are holding our book, it would be this: Help and ensure EVERYONE in your organization sees the mission and vision of the organization.

To do this you NEED to know the vision and mission of your organization. It needs to be a part of you, moved in way of commitment from your head to the very depths of your being.

One story illustrates this principle with power and simplicity. There was a group of young men who were part of a small non-profit organization. One of the members of their team was from El Salvador and living in the United States. In every way he was a smart and hardworking young man, but he struggled to learn the English language. The team tried to unite in a number of different ways, the whole time feeling this young man was on the same page as everyone else. One of the team members secured behind the scenes tickets to a large and prestigious aquarium. For weeks leading up to this team building event, team members would ask the young man from El Salvador if he was ready to see the Sharks, Dolphins, the Octopus, etc. He always answered yes and that he was really excited. On the day of the event everyone was talking about the trip and when the allotted time came to leave the office, part of the team piled in the car. As they were driving out of the parking lot, their young, Spanish speaking colleague asked the driver, confused, "Wait! Where are we going?"

He had never understood but his actions and responses had made it seem like he did. Yet, there was an obvious, even glaring disconnect. The mini mission was to build unity by sharing experiences at the aquarium, he had not even understood they were going to the aquarium. Language wasn't the issue, communication was the issue and the negative consequences of assuming you are understood. (You'll be happy to know that this young man is now an accomplished English interpreter and weekly radio host.)

Now this story is about a simple team building trip but you can easily see the correlation that can be made in the stories of countless organizations trying to establish a unified culture with everyone onboard. If even one person doesn't understand the mission and vision of the organization, no matter how well you think you've explained it, you will always be answering the question "Where are we going?".

Aligning Actions to Mission

There was a time when one of the members of The Allazo Group was on a hike with some friends in the vast redwoods of Northern California. The day was cool and clear and the nature, breathtaking. Along the hike the redwoods begin to block out the sun and the path became dark and unclear. There came a fork in the path that seemed critical. Luckily there was a sign with an arrow that pointed in the exact direction the hikers needed to take. On that path, the trees thinned, the sun returned, confidence was renewed and the way became clear.

As the hike came to its end, there was another fork in the path. From the onset it was relatively clear which way to take but as the group looked around for a sign with a directional arrow for confirmation, they found it had fallen over and been covered in moss. The arrow pointed to neither direction, only back into the woods. One of the hikers sarcastically remarked, "Well that's really helpful!" Another wisely stated, "You know, it's a good thing we had the fallen down sign here and the standing sign with the arrow pointing the right way at the last fork in the path and not the other way around." True statement. Despite the fallen down sign, the hikers made it back to the trailhead safe.

At The Allazo Group, we believe in arrows. There is an old Japanese legend brought to light at the introduction of the "Three Arrows" economic stimulus plan of Japan's Prime Minister, Shinzo Abe in 2013. The economic plan isn't the point here. The legend of the three arrows is. The legend finds its origin in the actions of a feudal warlord from West Japan, named Mori Motonari, born in 1497. According to legend, Motonari gave each of his three sons an arrow and told them to snap it in half. They each did with ease. After this initial exercise Motonari took out three arrows and asked each of his sons to try and snap all three at once. They could not, and as legend goes, Motonari, to instill the importance of teamwork on behalf of the kingdom, taught his sons that day that it is easy to break one arrow but it is nearly impossible to break three arrows at once.

The same legend applies to our organizations. One person alone facing in the right direction is powerful, but an entire team facing in the right direction is a real force to be reckoned with. In the following diagrams, imagine that every arrow represents a member of your organization.

Badly organized teams look something like this:

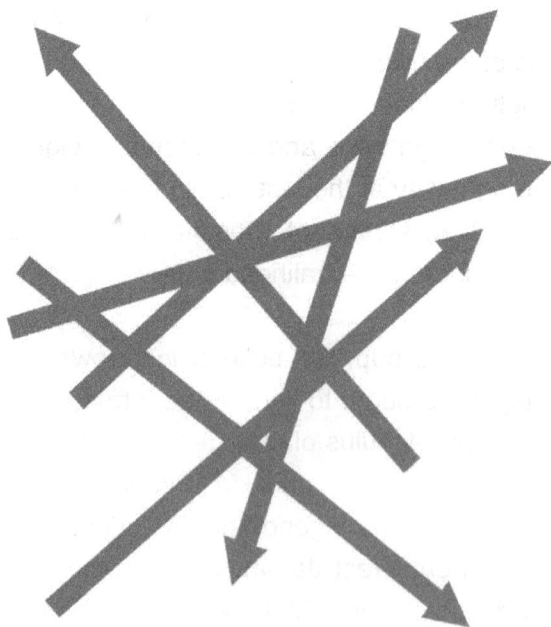

Most organizations look something like this.

The best organizations look something like this:

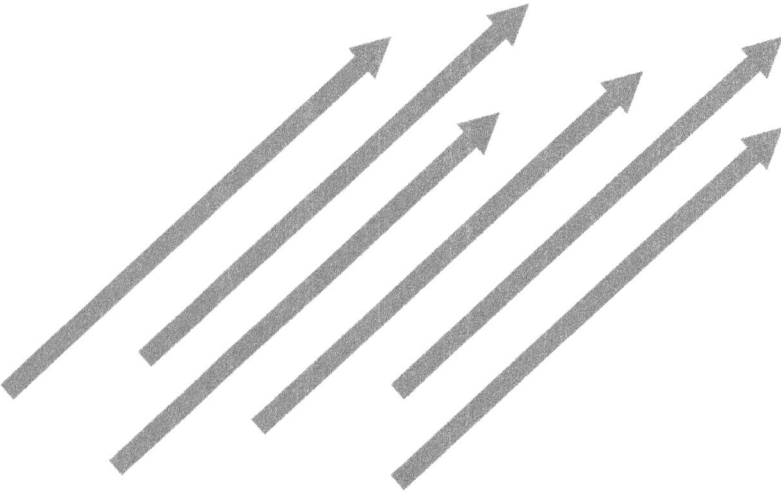

Arrows can also be seen as actions in our lives. If we are shooting our arrows in the right directions, towards our mission and goals, we are much more likely to succeed. Let's look at the same images but in this case, envision the arrows as decisions you make throughout your day, year or life.

This is where we run into problems.

Most of the time we look like this.

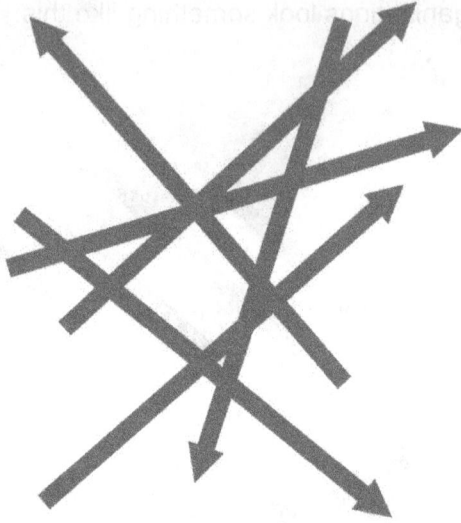

When we master our arrows, this is what our lives can look like:

What needs to be done for your team to have all its arrows pointing back to its mission? When you accomplish this, over and

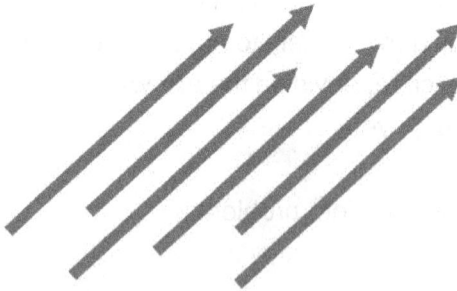

over again, you will find the unity necessary to move even higher in the Leadership Revolution.

_____

_____

_____

_____

_____

_____

_____

_____

_____

_____

When united like these arrows towards a common purpose, we are ready to elevate to the next turn in the revolution.

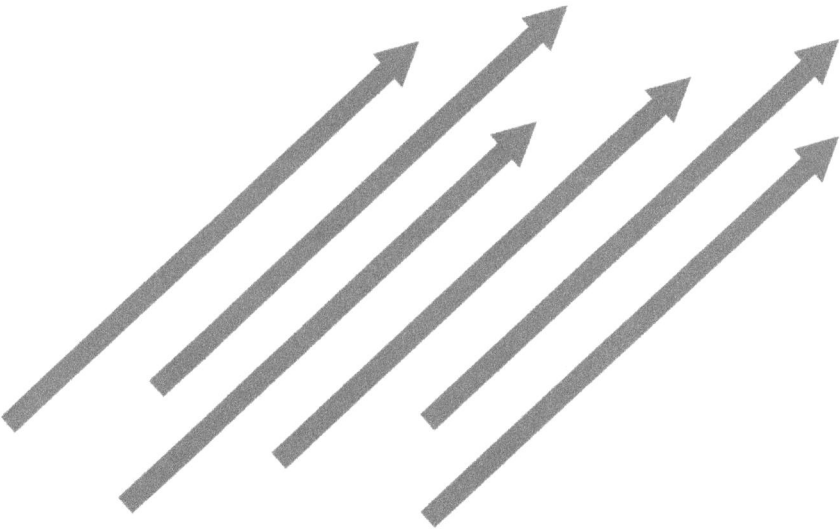

ELEVATE

Before we go any further, let's review what the cycle should look like and not look like.

The Main Leadership Cycle

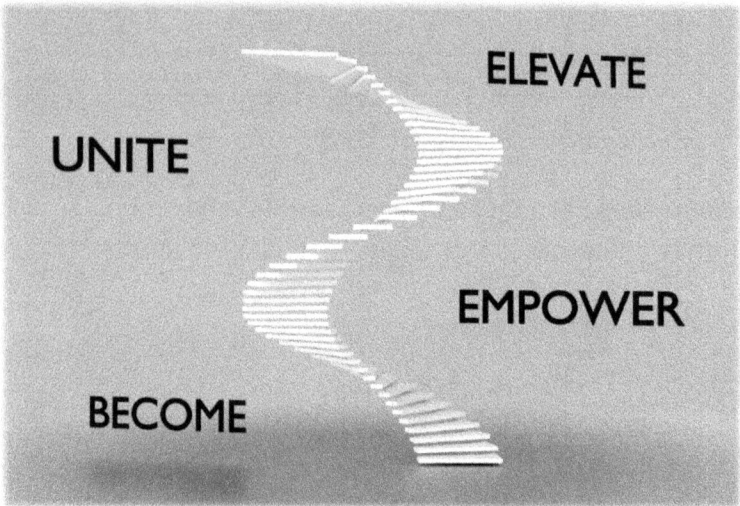

The Opposite of the Cycle

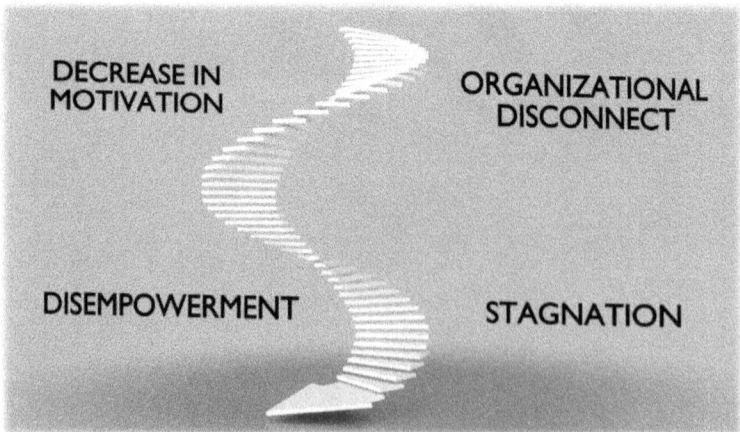

The goal is to move upward and not downward on our symbolic staircase and that the final piece of a revolution is to elevate back to Become. That is the mission. That is the quest. In the words of Francois de la Rochefoucauld, "There is a kind of elevation which does not depend on fortune; it is a certain air which distinguishes us, and seems to destine us for great things; it is a price we imperceptibly set upon ourselves." What price are we willing to pay for this air that distinguishes us?

What Does It Mean to Elevate?

One day a young man we know well was walking with his girlfriend up a steep and daunting hill towards the university they attended. It was a beautiful autumn day but the young man wouldn't have known it, his head was down in quiet determination to get to the top of the hill and to his awaiting classes. The young woman stopped and being hand in hand with the young man, stopped him as well. She forced eye contact and said, "You know what your problem is?" Defensively, the young man said, "What are you talking about?" But she continued, "You know what your problem is don't you?" Giving up the young man said, "Why don't you tell me." She smiled and said, "You never look up." "Of course I do!", said the young man becoming defensive for no real reason at all. She responded, "We walk up this same hill every day and you never look up. Close your eyes!" She demanded. The young man obediently closed his eyes. "What color are the leaves on the tree just above the path?" Trying to be clever but having no idea the young man said, "Just starting to change colors." She said, "That's what it looked like three weeks ago. Open your eyes and look up." Again he obeyed and looking up he saw the most breathtaking array of fluorescent red leaves dancing in the sunlight. They strode hand in hand, higher than they normally would have walked and took in the beauty that was mother nature. Turning to her boyfriend, the young woman said, "Isn't it amazing what you can see if you'll only look up?"

In essence, this story is what it means to elevate. It is to take what is working and make it better, more beautiful, to change perspective and thus change lives. The leadership of this young woman not only changed the young man's outlook on his daily walk up that hill but on his life, as he strived to be more observant, more patient and more grateful in his future leadership responsibilities. To elevate is to raise or lift something or someone up to a higher level or to raise them to a more important and impressive level. In the Leadership Revolution this is the solemn responsibility of every individual to both lift themselves, those around them and their entire organization to higher ground and states of mind, the likes of which they have never experienced before.

Elevated Organizations See Things Differently

Just as the young man in the story began to see his walk up that hill and began to view his priorities differently, elevated organizations see things differently with every turn upward in the staircase of leadership. This isn't to say they have entirely new views on leadership and organizational effectiveness, but they are constantly adding to their body of knowledge and their breadth of perspective. There are a few critical scenarios where organizations that have elevated to higher levels see and comprehend things very differently than the average organization.

- Elevated Organizations are Proactive in Seeing Crisis: The very best organizations know how to deal with crisis. But if team members feel like their work life is always in crisis, then it's not really a crisis, it's an organizational culture. The reason the best organizations know how to deal with crisis is because they are so proactive in avoiding crisis in the first place. Their employees see it coming down the road before anyone else, and they do everything in their power to steer clear of it.

- Elevated Organizations See Opportunity Quicker than Average Organizations: No one can see the future but great organizations not only read the trends of market but adapt to them before they arise. From preparing leaders to guide the most diverse of workplaces to being on the cutting edge of technology, the elevated organization always seems to be a step ahead. By preparing diligently through becoming, empowering to knowledge and uniting around a common cause, elevated organizations avoid the disaster described by Thomas Hardy, "There is a condition worse than blindness, and that is, seeing something that isn't there."

- Elevated Organizations are Consistent not Sporadic: "We are what we repeatedly do. Excellence, then, is not an act, but a habit." Aristotle said that, and it is as true today as it was in his time. Highly elevated organizations aren't just great one day and down the next, they have progressed to a point where excellence is just a part of their organizational culture. Consistency builds trust, consistency in excellence breeds more excellence. It starts over again every morning. In the response of the famous British soccer coach, Sir Bobby

Robson, when asked about the most important time in a soccer match, ""The first ninety minutes of a football match are the most important." Likewise, every leadership opportunity is the most important leadership opportunity.

3 Examples of Elevation

An Individual

Duke Paoa Kahinu Mokoe Hulikohola Kahanamoku, better known as Duke Kahanamoku or "The Big Kahuna" might be the greatest athlete and cultural icon you've never heard of.

After winning two gold medals in Stockholm in 1912 as a swimmer, the native Hawaiian turned to his true passion, surfing, to uncharted waters. He introduced the sport to the U.S. Atlantic Coast, Australia and New Zealand. He then began to popularize what became known as the "Surf Movement" in California. He went on to raise money for the World War One war effort by participating in swimming exhibitions in over thirty cities. He then continued by participating in several more Olympics, starred in movies and served as Sheriff in Honolulu.

Throughout Duke's life he lived the revolution, empowering and uniting along his way. He elevated a mere hobby to a coastal movement just by his example. He elevated a community to a life of fitness. He elevated a nation to support their troops. He elevated the newly found state of Hawaii to a level of fascination in the eyes of the lower Forty-Eight states.

One leader who walked many revolutions on the staircase of leadership. Sometimes it just takes one person with the vision of what could be, to make it so.

A Small Group

Everything seemed to be going well for the Apollo 13 mission to the moon, until the moment it didn't. The following is the story told directly by NASA. The text is filled with the four aspects of the Leadership Revolution. As you read, highlight, make note or underline them as you see them. We will leave room for you to record your findings at the end of NASA's report.

At 5 1/2 minutes after liftoff, John Swigert, Fred Haise and James Lovell felt a little vibration. Then the center engine of the S-II stage shut down two minutes early. This caused the remaining four engines to burn 34 seconds longer than planned, and the S-IVB third stage had to burn nine seconds longer to put Apollo 13 in orbit.

Days before the mission, backup lunar module pilot, Charles Duke, inadvertently exposed the crew to German measles. Command Module Pilot Ken Mattingly had no immunity to measles and was replaced by backup command module pilot, John Swigert.

Ground tests before launch indicated the possibility of a poorly insulated supercritical helium tank in the lunar module, or LM, descent stage, so the flight plan was modified to enter the LM three hours early in order to obtain an onboard readout of helium tank pressure.

The No. 2 oxygen tank, serial number 10024X-TA0009, had been previously installed in the service module of Apollo 10, but was removed for modification and damaged in the process. The tank was fixed, tested at the factory, installed in the Apollo 13 service module and tested again during the Countdown Demonstration Test at NASA's Kennedy Space Center beginning March 16, 1970. The tanks normally are emptied to about half full. No. 1 behaved all right, but No. 2 dropped to only 92 percent of capacity. Gaseous oxygen at 80 pounds per square inch was applied through the vent line to expel the liquid oxygen, but to no avail. An interim discrepancy report was written, and on March 27, two weeks before launch, detanking operations resumed. No. 1 again emptied normally, but No. 2 did not. After a conference with contractor and NASA personnel, the test director decided to "boil off" the remaining oxygen in No. 2 by using the electrical heater within the tank. The technique worked, but it took eight hours of 65-volt DC power from the ground support equipment to dissipate the oxygen. Due to an oversight in replacing an underrated component during a design modification, this turned out to severely damage the internal heating elements of the tank.

Apollo 13 was to be the third lunar landing attempt, but the mission was aborted after rupture of service module oxygen tank. Still, it was classified as a "successful failure" because of the experience gained in rescuing the crew. The mission's spent upper stage successfully impacted the moon.

During the first two days, the crew ran into a couple of minor surprises, but generally Apollo 13 was looking like the smoothest flight of the program. At 46 hours, 43 minutes Joe Kerwin, the capsule communicator, or Capcom, on duty, said, "The spacecraft is in real good shape as far as we are concerned. We're bored to tears down here." It was the last time anyone would mention boredom for a long time.

At 55 hours, 46 minutes, as the crew finished a 49-minute TV broadcast showing how comfortably they lived and worked in weightlessness, Lovell said, "This is the crew of Apollo 13 wishing everybody there a nice evening, and we're just about ready to close out our inspection of Aquarius and get back for a pleasant evening in Odyssey. Good night."

Nine minutes later, oxygen tank No. 2 blew up, causing the No. 1 tank to also fail. The command module's normal supply of electricity, light and water was lost, and they were about 200,000 miles from Earth.

The message came in the form of a sharp bang and vibration at 9:08 p.m. April 13. Swigert saw a warning light that accompanied the bang and said, "Houston, we've had a problem here." Lovell came on and told the ground that it was a main B bus undervolt.

Next, the warning lights indicated the loss of two of three fuel cells, which were the spacecraft's prime source of electricity. With warning lights blinking, one oxygen tank appeared to be completely empty and there were indications that the oxygen in the second tank was rapidly depleting.

Thirteen minutes after the explosion, Lovell happened to look out of the left-hand window and saw the final evidence pointing toward potential catastrophe. "We are venting something out into the... into space," he reported to Houston. Capcom Jack Lousma replied, "Roger, we copy you venting." Lovell said, "It's a gas of some sort." It was oxygen gas escaping at a high rate from the second, and last, oxygen tank.

The first thing the crew did, even before discovering the oxygen leak, was try to close the hatch between the CM and the LM. They reacted spontaneously, similar to a submarine crew, closing the hatches to limit the amount of flooding. First Swigert, and then Lovell, tried to lock the reluctant hatch, but the stubborn lid wouldn't stay shut. Exasperated and realizing that there wasn't a cabin leak, they strapped the hatch to the CM couch.

The pressure in the No. 1 oxygen tank continued to drift downward; passing 300 pounds per square inch, then headed toward 200 pounds per square inch. Months later, after the accident investigation was complete, it was determined that when the No. 2 tank blew up, it either ruptured a line on the No. 1 tank or caused one of the valves to leak. When the pressure reached 200 pounds per square inch, the crew and ground controllers knew they would lose all oxygen, which meant that the last fuel cell also would die.

At one hour, 29 seconds after the bang, Lousma said after instructions from Flight Director Glynn Lunney, "It is slowly going to zero, and we are starting to think about the LM lifeboat." Swigert replied, "That's what we have been thinking about too."

Ground controllers in Houston faced a formidable task. Completely new procedures had to be written and tested in the simulator before being passed up to the crew. The navigation problem had to be solved; essentially how, when and in what attitude to burn the LM descent engine to provide a quick return home.

With only 15 minutes of power left in the CM, Lousma told the crew to make their way into the LM. Haise and Lovell quickly floated through the tunnel, leaving Swigert to perform the last chores in the command module. The first concern was to determine if there were enough consumables to get home. The LM was built for only a 45-hour lifetime and it needed to be stretch to 90. Oxygen wasn't a problem. The full LM descent tank alone would suffice. In addition, there were two ascent-engine oxygen tanks and two backpacks full of oxygen that would never be used on the lunar surface. Two emergency bottles on top of those packs each had six or seven pounds in them. At LM jettison just before re-entry 28.5 pounds of oxygen remained, more than half of what was available after the explosion.

Power also was a concern. There were 2,181 ampere hours in the LM batteries. Ground controllers carefully worked out a procedure where the CM batteries were charged with LM power. All noncritical systems were turned off and energy consumption was reduced to 1/5, which resulted in having 20 percent of LM electrical power left when Aquarius was jettisoned. There was one electrical close call during the mission. One of the CM batteries vented with such force that it momentarily dropped off the line. Had the battery failed, there would have been insufficient power to return the ship to Earth.

Water was the main consumable concern. It was estimated that the crew would run out of water about five hours before Earth re-entry, which was calculated at around 151 hours. However, data from Apollo 11, which had not sent its LM ascent stage crashing into the moon as in subsequent missions, showed that its mechanisms could survive seven or eight hours in space without water cooling. The crew conserved water. They cut down to six ounces each per day, 1/5 of normal intake, and used fruit juices; they ate hot dogs and other wet-pack foods when they ate at all. The crew became dehydrated throughout the flight and set a record that stood up throughout Apollo: Lovell lost 14 pounds and the crew lost a total of 31.5 pounds, nearly 50 percent more than any other crew. Those stringent measures resulted in the crew finishing with 28.2 pounds of water, about 9 percent of the total.

Removal of carbon dioxide also was a concern. There were enough lithium hydroxide canisters, which remove carbon dioxide from the spacecraft, but the square canisters from the command module were not compatible with the round openings in the lunar module environmental system. There were four cartridges from the LM and four from the backpacks, counting backups. However, the LM was designed to support two men for two days and was being asked to care for three men for about four days. After a day and a half in the LM, a warning light showed that the carbon dioxide had built up to a dangerous level. Mission control devised a way to attach the CM canisters to the LM system by using plastic bags, cardboard and to tape all materials carried on board.

One of the big questions was, "How to get back safely to Earth?" The LM navigation system wasn't designed to help in this situation. Before the explosion at 30 hours, 40 minutes, Apollo 13 had made the normal midcourse correction, which would take it out of a free-return-to-Earth trajectory and put it on a lunar landing course. Now the task was to get back on a free-return course. The ground computed a 35-second burn and fired it five hours after the explosion. As they approached the moon, another burn was computed; this time a long five-minute burn to speed up the return home. It took place two hours after rounding the far side of the moon.

The command module navigational platform alignment was transferred to the LM, but verifying alignment was difficult. Ordinarily the alignment procedure uses an onboard sextant device, called the Alignment Optical Telescope, or AOT, to find a suitable navigation star. Then with the help of an onboard computer, it verifies the guidance platform's alignment. However, due to the explosion, a swarm of debris from the ruptured service module made it impossible to sight real stars. An alternate procedure was developed to use the sun as an alignment star. Lovell rotated the spacecraft to the attitude Houston had requested and when he looked through the AOT, the sun was just where it was expected. The alignment with the sun proved to be less than 1/2 a degree off. The ground and crew then knew they could do the five-minute P.C. + 2 burn with assurance, cutting the total time of their voyage to about 142 hours. At 73 hours, 46 minutes into the mission, the air-to-ground transcript describes the event:

Lovell: OK. We got it. I think we got it. What diameter was it?

Haise: Yes. It's coming back in. Just a second.

Lovell: Yes, yaw's coming back in. Just about it.

Haise: Yaw is in....

Lovell: What have you got?

Haise: Upper-right corner of the sun....

Lovell: We've got it! If we raised our voices, I submit it was justified.

Flight Director Gerald Griffin, a man not easily shaken, recalled: "Some years later I went back to the log and looked up that mission. My writing was almost illegible; I was so damned nervous. And I remember the exhilaration running through me: My God, that's the last hurdle - if we can do that, I know we can make it. It was funny because only the people involved knew how important it was to have that platform properly aligned." Yet Griffin barely mentioned the alignment in his change-of-shift briefing - "That check turned out real well" is all he said an hour after his penmanship failed him.

The trip was marked by discomfort beyond the lack of food and water. Sleep was almost impossible because of the cold. When the electrical systems were turned off, the spacecraft lost an important source of heat. The temperature dropped to 38 degrees Fahrenheit and condensation formed on all the walls.

The most remarkable achievement of mission control was quickly developing procedures for powering up the CM after its long, cold sleep. Flight controllers wrote the documents for this innovation in three days, instead of the usual three months. The command module was cold and clammy at the start of power-up. The walls, ceiling, floor, wire harnesses and panels were all covered with droplets of water. It was suspected conditions were the same behind the panels. The chances of short circuits caused apprehension, but thanks to the safeguards built into the command module after the disastrous Apollo 1 fire in January 1967, no arcing took place. Lovell recalled the descent to Earth, "The droplets furnished one sensation as we decelerated in the atmosphere: it rained inside the CM."

Four hours before landing, the crew shed the service module; mission control had insisted on retaining it until then because everyone feared what the cold of space might do to the un-sheltered CM heat shield. Photos of the service module showed one whole panel missing and wreckage hanging out, it was a mess as it drifted away. Three hours later, the crew left the lunar module Aquarius and then splashed down gently in the Pacific Ocean near Samoa.

What aspects of the Leadership Revolution stood out to you the most in this report?

_____

_____

_____

_____

_____

_____

_____

_____

A Team

A new manager had the privilege of working with a large and young group of aspiring professionals. They were traveling across the country making presentations on the products their company produced. This led them into the heart of a small town in Kansas where they were scheduled to stay the night.

The young manager had made it a point to be consistent in his expectations and his actions with his inexperienced yet enthusiastic cohort. He held weekly meetings with each member of his team, a tiring task, to empower them and discuss their roles, strengths and to encourage them in every aspect of their life, not just their work. He also held daily meetings to promote unity amongst a large group that came from different parts of the country, with different experiences and backgrounds.

Over time this inspired an unprecedented level of confidence and trust in their leader. That night in Kansas a siren went off and a warning came over the news. A massive tornado was tearing through Kansas and heading directly for their motel.

Now in regards to the Leadership Revolution, week by week this young manager had ascended upward, but in this time of panic, the trust and confidence his team had developed in him led to an elevated level of leadership that is only earned, not taken.

He turned to his co-manager and tasked him to find a shelter and report back to him. He found three leaders amongst the group with strengths he knew from personal experience after all of those interviews, and put them in charge of different members of the team. They then went out and found water, food and supplies.

No one in that group had ever been through a tornado. It would have been reasonable if some of them had even panicked; but they did not. They elevated. They elevated because of the steady and committed leadership of their manager and mentor. That young team rose to the occasion, unified their efforts and got through the night safely.

What will you do today, this week and this month to elevate your team?

_____

_____

_____

_____

_____

_____

_____

_____

_____

_____

_____

_____

_____

_____

_____

What it Takes to Make the Cycle Work at Its Full Potential

To make sure the Leadership Cycle is working like a well-oiled machine we have to understand the components that make it run. Only then can you complete the Revolution and ascend to the next level of leadership efficiency. We once visited a man who had classic books sitting in his library. We asked him which one impacted him most. He responded with a title but then said, "but that's also the only one I've read." Apparently he had never made the time for the books or the impact they could have had on him. Instead the books and their lessons just sat on a shelf gathering dust. There are numerous important things we can do to make sure the cycle is working at as its full potential. Crucial principles include:

Time Management

Time is the only commodity we are given each day in equal proportion. No matter how hard we work, we only get twenty-four hours in a day and so do you. Those twenty-four hours are yours and yours alone. You get to decide what to do with them. In essence the moments that make up the minutes that make up the hours ultimately determine what kind of leader you become.

So if you want to be a unifying leader, make a plan to proactively go out and give yourself the time to become that unifying leader. In the words of the Yankee great, Yogi Berra, who left us far too soon at the age of 90, "If you don't know where you are going, you'll end up someplace else." Without the time or vision to become, empower and unify, you will be hard pressed to become what you need to become, empower who you need to empower and unite the team that needs to be united.

Perhaps this is best illustrated in a quote by Victor Hugo. "He who every morning plans the transaction of the day and follows out that plan, carries a thread that will guide him through the maze of the busiest life. But where no plan is laid, where the disposal of time is surrendered merely to the chance of incidence, chaos will soon reign." Flexibility is ok, but it can't be an excuse for creating a plan that will allow you to have the time necessary to do the things you MUST do.

We recommend an A,B,C system, easily remembered with the acronym "Always Be Consistent". Always be consistent in putting the most important things first. Always be consistent in following the steps of the Leadership Revolution. Always be consistent in aligning your actions with your vision.

Here is a simple breakdown of how this planning system works and how easy it becomes to keep your life organized when you are consistent!

The A, B, C System
A = Absolute   B = Beneficial   C = Convenient

Planning is essential but planning is more than just having a general idea of what you might be doing over the next six months. In comes the A, B, C system. Always Be Consistent! Start with your main goal, to fulfill the mission of your organization and have that in mind as you go through the planning process either in the morning as your day starts or at night when your day ends.

Your A's are the things that have to be done TODAY, no matter what, no excuses. These are the things that simply cannot be done tomorrow and are essential to not just fulfilling the organization's mission but to maintain the existence of the organization!

Your B's are the things that really ought to be done today but are legitimately ok to put off until tomorrow. If you get past you A's, work through your B's. Likely some of your B's today are going to be your A's tomorrow. On a bigger scale, if you are planning three months in advance for example, your B's will be essential things you need to think about and plan for but will likely be executed a couple weeks out.

Your C's are things that need to be done but are not essential at the moment. On a daily list, you can call it a really successful day if you get through your A's and B's. If you get to the C's just call yourself lucky. C's become B's eventually, the same way B's become A's.

If you stick to this system, you will get A LOT done. More than you have probably ever done before. Why? Because you will stop spending all your time on irrelevant C tasks and instead free up time to empower and unite.

Start every project by listing off your A's, B's and C's and then every day listing off your A's, B's and C's. This will allow you to see how effective you are and also keep you from falling into the trap of spending hours and hours on non-essential things.

Here is how a daily list might look for a leader in the role of a principal:

A

A: Personally meet with every department chair, respond to their requests and proactively get them on board for the staff meeting. (The highest energy task are best at the beginning of the day when you have the most energy!)

A: Attend Staff Meeting at 8:30AM, Speak no more than fifteen minutes. (Obviously has to be done today)

A: Finish report for Superintendent with updated staff meeting minutes.

B

B: Visit Ms. Johnson's English Class (Promised it would be done by the end of the week, a good "B" item.)

B: Review new lunch procedures document and make revisions (due in two days.)

C

C: Make proactive phone calls to parents whose students are struggling, offer support and insights.

C: Start next week's math department class visits.

As you can see, your A's are appointments for the day and things that simply cannot be put off. For example, you know booking the auditorium any later than today will likely mean you won't have the auditorium for your event.

Your two's are important but can wait until tomorrow if needed. Your threes are the things that need to be done, but can be about a week out if you don't get to them sooner. It takes discipline to create a list every day for your work life, but over the long run it does nothing but pay off.

For many, it's a good idea to break these lists up into shorter lists, one for work, one for family and one for a number of other categories that you choose to use in those twenty-four hours we have all been allotted. You can also make these lists according to categories of your organization, time allotment, your energy levels, people you need to meet with, etc. Remember, these lists exist to help you free up your time for the things and more importantly, the people, that matter most. When you are at work be a uniter, when you come home be at home and love, empower and unite there just as much as you would at work. Let's take a look at what an A,B,C list might look like for your family time. Remember in some cases, as in the case of this example, your A's, B's and C's are simply for the night and in order of priority not to be renewed throughout the week. You will need to start this type of list over nightly!

Family Time

A: Attend Son's basketball game tonight at 7pm, be there at 6:30 so he can see me watching him warm up.

A: Take the family out for ice cream after the game (Friday night family activity).

A: Bring wife flowers since we only have five minutes of alone time before we meet our daughter at the game.

B: Straighten up picture at the center of living room with a level. (Could wait till Saturday)

B: Put in load of laundry I collected this morning before rushing out the door. (No one is in desperate need of it, but it would be good to get it done.)

C: Catch up on Netflix series I started last week.

As you can see, PEOPLE come first. Tasks that help those people you love come second and will easily find a place in the "A" group when the timing is right. Your "C's" if you are doing things right will be "C's" for a while, but they will find their time and place. Remember, there are countless things you COULD do in this kind of reinventing daily list, but there are only a few things you SHOULD do. Make time for what matters most, or what matters most will not likely make time for you.

One final thought on time management we all need to remember. It is impossible to function at your highest capacity if your mind and energy are split exponentially into an endless number of tasks that "must be done." Mastering your mind and disciplining your time is the only true way to harness the power behind your best intentions. Discipline is focus, but like the sun, focus brings the concentration of your greatest light and therefore, your greatest abilities.

Accountability

If, in your mind, the Leadership Revolution is just another program that will come and go, it will fail. You must be accountable for your own becoming. That is on you. No one else can control it, no one else should be so invested in it as you. It' the same as your happiness, Esther Hicks, author of nine books on the subject wrote, "If you knew your potential to feel good, you would ask no one to be different so that you can feel good. You would free yourself of all of that cumbersome impossibility of needing to control the world, or control your mate, or control your child. You are the only one who creates your reality. For no one else can think for you, no one else can do it. It is only you, every bit of it you."

At the same time, as you seek to empower others and you are taking the time to guide them, they must be accountable for the actions they pledge to take. If they come back to you having done nothing, changed nothing and became nothing and then you do nothing, what message does that send? That your time is worth nothing.

In regards to unity, one quick way to ruin the trust of those around you and in the Revolution is to bring it up once with excitement, let it be a theme for a week and then don't bring it up again for a week. Consistently be consistent and let the benefits flow consistently. People hear the word accountability and immediately think "reprimand". That is only the case if you make it that way. If you choose to make it a time of encouragement and growth, the word takes on an entirely different meaning.

Constantly Check In

Make the rhetoric of the Leadership Revolution a part of your everyday language. This will, in fact, elevate your thoughts, actions and desires to a higher level because you will inadvertently be focused on the most crucial aspects of leadership.

Take self-inventory of where you are in the revolution. Take inventory of where others are as well. Don't be afraid of the answers, a good reality check is nothing but a measuring stick and a benchmark on which to base improvement. In the words of author Lev Grossman, "If there's a single lesson that life teaches us, it's that wishing doesn't make it so." You can call a cat a dog but it's not. You can call a stalled company progressing and it's not. Don't let ignorance contort your organizational intelligence, by constantly checking in, you will know exactly how the Revolution is progressing and how you can help more of your team to progress upwards to their highest potential.

Creating a Culture of Excellence

Cultures of excellence come in organizations of all shapes and sizes. Despite their population, geographical and industry differences, they share certain traits that facilitate excellence in their craft. You might be asking; how do I create that kind of culture? The answer is this... We have already given you the answer. The answer is contained in the previous pages of this book. Knowing all organizations are different and knowing they stand in different steps scattered throughout the spiral staircase, the answer is different for everyone, including all of us at the Allazo Group. Thinking of your leadership situation and reviewing the timeless principles of the Leadership Revolution, what would you say are the components specific to you and your team in creating a lasting culture of excellence?

_____
_____
_____
_____
_____
_____
_____
_____
_____
_____
_____
_____
_____
_____

If you are having trouble getting started, here are some standards that you might want to include:

- Create Extremely United Teams
- Work Towards a Common Vision
- Make Sure Everyone Understands The Mission
- Help Others to Master Their Roles and Conquer New Roles
- Give Meaning to Everything You Do
- Provide An Opportunity For Constant Support And Sharing

Sometimes creating or even maintaining a culture of excellence comes from doing things that are unthinkable at the time, but are looked back upon as trend setting. An example that resonates to the core of selfless elevation of a nation is the story of George Washington.

As written by Ron Chernow in Washington; a Life, referring to the day of Washington's and America's first inauguration...

Washington knew that everything he did at the swearing-in would establish a tone for the future. "As the first of everything in *our situation* will serve to establish a precedent," he reminded Madison, "it is devoutly wished on my part that these precedents may be fixed on true principles." He would shape indelibly the institution of the presidency. Although he had earned his reputation in battle, he made a critical decision not to wear a uniform at the inauguration or beyond, banishing fears of a military coup. Instead, he would stand there aglitter with patriotic symbols. To spur American manufactures, he would wear a double-breasted brown suit, made from broadcloth woven at the Woolen Manufactory of Hartford, Connecticut. The suit had gilt buttons with an eagle insignia on them; to round out his outfit, he would wear white hosiery, silver shoe buckles and yellow gloves. Washington already sensed that Americans would emulate their presidents. "I hope it will not be a great while before it will be unfashionable for a gentleman to appear in any other dress," he told his friend the Marquis de Lafayette, referring to his American attire. "Indeed, we have already been too long subject to British prejudices." To burnish his image further on Inauguration Day, Washington would powder his hair and wear a dress sword on his hip, sheathed in a steel scabbard."

Excellence begins in the mind. Washington understood that in order to elevate the new nation over which he was to preside, they first needed to elevate their thoughts to a new way of thinking. He exemplified this elevated thought process throughout his presidency, stair upon stair, until a culture was established on which others could build. This culminated in Washington doing the unthinkable, stepping down after two terms in office, setting an example only he could set and clearly sending the message that no man or woman's power was or should ever be above that of the people they are sworn to serve.

What it Takes to Change Culture

It wasn't that long ago that we met with a friend and former colleague who recently became the manager of a large and diverse group of employees. His team was experienced, talented and accomplishing great things. This ultimately led to a sense of complacency and resistance to our friends push to see from a higher vista. He explained to us that much of his struggle lies in helping the team create a new organizational culture that keeps all the good from the existing culture while allowing them to grow into the greater vision they need. Only this will allow them to progress smoothly into the opportunities of the future.

Our friend is not alone in this struggle. It is hard to shake the old way of doing things even when a better way is clear. The process of changing the culture of any organization can be a daunting task.

Yet it has been done before and there are several key things our friend can do to enhance the process of his organizational culture change.

1. Reinforce the vision and mission: As you know, a vision statement is a formal statement of organizational philosophy, it is the big picture of what an organization plans to achieve over time. It is a short, powerful statement that should apply to ALL members of the organization from the highest manager to the janitorial staff and should be easily repeated by any employee at any given time.

The mission statement defines the present purpose of the organization. It should cover what the organization does and what it stands for, how it accomplishes its goals and who it provides its services to.

Employees should be able to look at both the vision and mission statements as a guide on how to make decisions within the organization and clearly understand where the organization stands and where their individual efforts should ultimately lead.

A leader can bring a new perspective to an existing mission. They can create opportunities for their team to not just hear but experience this new perspective.

2. Attack from every angle: It is not enough to stand up and give a speech on the importance of the new way of doing things. A speech is a starting point but the message should be driven home from every angle of the organization. The way the office is designed, the art on the walls, the slogans used in the organization, the stories told in meetings, the conversations had throughout the day should all be an example of the new positive culture being created.

3. Deliberate Role Modeling: Leaders at every level should be the highest examples of the new culture they desire to create. If there is disunity amongst senior leadership, any organizational culture changing effort will fail. Their interactions with their employees should reflect the highest ideals of the organization. They must become what they are teaching. Be responsible for ensuring what is done each day is actually compatible with where the organization needs to go. Disconnect between the day to day efforts and ultimate vision will crush any culture changing effort. Consistent coaching, follow up and personal interactions are all powerful tools in changing culture.

4. Focused Training: Too many organizations feel a single large training will suffice in changing culture. They then move on to other topics. This is an unproductive strategy. The ideals, goals and behavior associated with the new culture need to be the subject of every training! The principles need to be driven home again and again, from diverse angles and with practical application until they are no longer the exception but the norm.

5. Help your team see why: We have discussed "Why and Transparency" but it is more than worth mentioning again. If people can't see why a culture change is necessary and beneficial, they will likely never change. Helping the team catch the vision of the why behind the change, the ultimate possibilities for both them and the organization is crucial. Remind them of the why and the what and the how will be more readily received. Explain the what and how without the why and your efforts will likely fail.

Helping an organization to achieve a new, more productive, service oriented culture is a noble cause. It is these kinds of culture changes that have far reaching impacts on organizations and their members. They are the stuff of ascending step by step to higher levels. Through sustained planning and effort this type of transformation is not only possible but greatly enhances the organization's opportunities for long term, sustainable success in the Leadership Revolution.

Bring in Pieces That Fit Once Culture is Established

Once your culture is established and the course of your organization is that of a consistent upward ascension by every member of your team, then protecting that positive culture should be one of your very highest priorities. The way to protect that culture that controls so much of your organization's potential lies in a step by step method taught to us by a seasoned organizational practitioner from the great state of Arizona. Her process is as follows:

To honor her we will call it Murphy's Other Law - Of Creating a Sustainable Organizational Culture:

1. Accurately and as unbiased as possible determine the REAL culture of your organization. What is said by organizational members in describing culture isn't usually the reality of the day in and day out situation. Observing words, behavior, practices and procedures are most likely to reveal true culture.

2. Determine the goals and desires of key shareholders. Where do you want to go? What's the vision? Why do you want to go there? What and who are holding the team back from accomplishing those goals?

3. Get buy in from those with the most influence using the principles taught previously.

4. Determine why certain practices and people are holding the team back. Is it a lack of understanding? Is it inadequate training?

5. Create a rubric and allow members to reflect on where they are on the rubric at different times and interactions. This creates a clear document with expectations for each member of the team.

6. Spend time training and allowing time for reflection for the team members. Stretch all shareholders to better themselves on the rubric, aim for being the best they can be.

7. Give valuable feedback with evidence so team members can honestly see where they are and how they can grow.

8. Recognize those around you and let them understand they are valuable.

9. After adequate time to change and improve, layout an improvement plan based on the rubric. If things don't change in the prescribed time, invite them to find a better organizational fit. In this way no one is ever surprised when asked to move on.

10. Search diligently and don't give up until a candidate is found that fits in with the new established organizational culture.

No one has done more work on the subject of "Getting the right people into your organization" than Jim Collins. He describes the process like this drawing from the work of another great organizational theorist, John C. Maxwell. "You are a bus driver. The bus, your company, is at a standstill, and it's your job to get it going. You have to decide where you're going, how you're going to get there, and who's going with you.

Most people assume that great bus drivers (read: business leaders) immediately start the journey by announcing to the people on the bus where they're going—by setting a new direction or by articulating a fresh corporate vision.

In fact, leaders of companies that go from good to great start not with "where" but with "who." They start by getting the right people on the bus, the wrong people off the bus, and the right people in the right seats. And they stick with that discipline—first the people, then the direction—no matter how dire the circumstances. Take David Maxwell's bus ride. When he became CEO of Fannie Mae in 1981, the company was losing $1 million every business day, with $56 billion worth of mortgage loans underwater. The board desperately wanted to know what Maxwell was going to do to rescue the company.

Maxwell responded to the "what" question the same way that all good-to-great leaders do: He told them, That's the wrong first question. To decide where to drive the bus before you have the right people on the bus, and the wrong people off the bus, is absolutely the wrong approach."

Get the right group of people on the bus. If people don't want to be a part of that group of the right people with the right attitudes and talents, invite them to find a new bus. Once everyone is standing on the bus, do not underestimate the importance of making sure those prepared and talented people are in the right seats!

One story that illustrates this point... A young graduate from one of the best universities in the United States was hired by perhaps the most prestigious business firms in the world. His talent was off the charts and his character impeccable. On paper, it was, in every way, a perfect fit! Because of his integrity he was asked to work in accounting. His passion was in advertising. He spoke to this many times in his performance reviews but his honest requests fell on deaf ears. After a year and a half of spectacular work and raving reviews by his superiors, he abruptly quit and eventually found his way to a startup that offered him drastically less pay and far less prestige but gave him the opportunity to be in advertising. A classic example of the right person on the bus sitting in the wrong seat with a driver unaware of what was going on behind them.

Share Success and Knowledge

A true ascension in the leadership revolution, your journey upward on that spiral staircase to the pantheon of effective leadership, cannot come without bringing others with you. In this metaphor, the stairs should be full of people walking together, stopping to take in the views, gaining new perspective with every turn. There are also those, leading out in front, those encouraging people from the back, others extending their hand encouraging a colleague to take one more step, to push a little bit farther into the depth of their potential.

In your own quest to make every day your masterpiece, you will inevitably inspire those around you to create their own crowning work one day of purpose at a time. There is no secret that the greatest joy in life is in helping others succeed. There is something special about being able to celebrate the successes of others as if they were your own. We can call this compassion but we can also call it trust, the kind of trust that comes from empowering and uniting through something bigger than your individual job or deadline. The real secret organization's fail to grasp is that bottom line success comes more easily, more cheerfully and with more sustainability the same way; by elevating a culture of I help you, you help me, we all help each other, and our company succeeds.

To create a culture that transcends the all too often opposite of the words above, or in other words, I stab you, you stab me, we don't trust each other, and our company falls into a pit of irrelevance, takes sustained effort. But then again, that's what we have been talking about this whole book, have we not? The steps are simple, they aren't rocket science, but to a rocket scientist with no vision of what their leadership stewardship entails, they may not be that simple.

Success is found in following the revolution, putting more trust into those around you and the system with every passing cycle. It is becoming your best, empowering others to do the same, uniting everyone around that idea of we are good and WILL be better and then doing it again, this time with more pristine focus, this time with even more enthusiasm, with growing numbers with an even more deeply committed team.

A few suggestions that will help that necessity to happen:

1. Create departmental conversations and encourage collective knowledge. This may come with some sacrifice of "conventional" work time, but it's dividends will be more than worth the change of pace.

2. Create tools for collaboration. Google docs, company wikies, open email services, newsletters, you name it, they will help spread knowledge. One warning, take the time to review these technologies to ensure that which is being shared is both true and effective!

3. Encourage question asking. This can come through an open door policy, in department meetings, through email and in a number of other ways. Comfort in asking questions = A higher level of knowledge obtained.

4. Share what you observe. In formal and informal settings, share your observations with team members. Record those observations and follow up with those same members to let them know you not only care about their progress but are there to help.

5. Keep track of the right stories and share them often. Stories are a powerful tool in passing along knowledge. Stories are also more likely to stick in the minds of your team members than a list of even the most relevant facts and figures.

6. Share resources. Physical workplaces, human capital, new perspectives and technologies. Think of "this is ours" as a statement encompassing the whole organization and not just fractions of it.

7. Value Social Media. With an ever changing workforce and organizational structures, social media is playing in ever increasing role in communication. For many it's the most convenient and familiar form of communication to team members. Harness that power to share knowledge, such as a Facebook "Successes Page" or a Twitter account that will allow your team members to follow you and the best practices you observe throughout the week.

No matter what strategies you choose, choose also to be consistent. In Buddha's words, "There is no wealth like knowledge and no poverty like ignorance." Choose to let others around you bask in that wealth. Knowledge is a precious resource, one that can easily be lost in a single organizational generation by simple complacency.

In the work of Kinicki and Colgate, they break down the need for Shared Human Capital.

Strategic assumption: People, Individually and collectivity, are the key to organizational success.

Strategic assumption: People, Individually and collectivity, are the key to organizational success.

Individual Human Capital	Social Capital
• Intelligence/abilities/knowledge • Visions/dreams/aspirations • Technical and social skills • Confidence/self esteem • Initiative/entrepreneurship • Adaptability/flexibility • Readiness to learn • Creativity • Enthusiasm • Motivation/commitment • Persistence • Ethical standards/courage • Honesty • Emotional maturity	• -Shared visions and goals • Shared values • Trust • Mutual respect/goodwill • Friendship/support groups • Mentoring/positive roles • Participation/empowerment • Connections/sources • Network/ affiliations • Cooperation/collaboration • Teamwork • Camaraderie • Assertive (rather than aggressive) communication • Functional (rather than dysfunctional) conflict • Win-win negotiations • Philanthropy/volunteering

Within these two forms of human capital consist points of connection where shared knowledge can take place.

Operating under the observation of George Bernard Shaw, that "the problem with communication... is the illusion it has been accomplished." With that said, what communication techniques can you apply to ensure there is more actual communication of knowledge taking place as opposed to the assumption it is taking place?

_____

_____

_____

_____

_____

_____

_____

_____

_____

_____

Elevate Always

We must always look to elevate. As people will undoubtedly be united, they will also be in different positions ascending the spiral staircase. The point is not to have everyone on the same step, but to have everyone consistently moving upward. Moving upward is changing, changing for good. From a man named William Pollard, who lived over 100 years ago, "Without change there is no innovation, creativity, or incentive for improvement. Those who initiate change will have a better opportunity to manage the change that is inevitable." By looking to elevate always, you are, in fact, initiating the change that will change your organization and ascend it to the next level.

The idea of doing what others hesitate to do is not a new concept. We have heard the poem by Robert Frost that preach the timeless words,

"Two roads diverged in a yellow wood,
And sorry I could not travel both
And be one traveler, long I stood
And looked down one as far as I could
To where it bent in the undergrowth;

Then took the other, as just as fair,
And having perhaps the better claim
Because it was grassy and wanted wear,
Though as for that the passing there
Had worn them really about the same,

And both that morning equally lay
In leaves no step had trodden black.
Oh, I kept the first for another day!
Yet knowing how way leads on to way
I doubted if I should ever come back.

I shall be telling this with a sigh
Somewhere ages and ages hence:
Two roads diverged in a wood, and I,
I took the one less traveled by,
And that has made all the difference"

Certainly the path of the Leadership Revolution, though beautiful in its simplicity, is still somehow the road less traveled by that will, without a doubt, make all the difference. But let's look together at another poem by Frost. Less known, less read but incredible in the promoting of the idea of Always Looking to Elevate better than just about any piece of literature;

Stopping by the Woods on a Snowy Evening

"Whose woods these are I think I know.
His house is in the village though;
He will not see me stopping here
To watch his woods, fill up with snow.

My little horse must think it queer
To stop without a farmhouse near
Between the woods and frozen lake
The darkest evening of the year.

He gives his harness bells a shake
To ask if there is some mistake.
The only other sound's the sweep
Of easy wind and downy flake.

The woods are lovely, dark and deep,
But I have promises to keep,
And miles to go before I sleep,
And miles to go before I sleep."

Sometimes in life and in leadership, it is easy to be distracted by the snow, the daunting nature of the task, the temptation to give in. Maybe the snow represented death, or in our case, complacency.

Maybe it was simply a brief moment to admire the beauty, but whatever the interpretation, there are the timeless lines that so eloquently recapitulate your duty to elevate.

> "But I have promises to keep,
> And miles to go before I sleep,
> And miles to go before I sleep."

Your promise is to help everyone around you to become, be empowered, unite as a team and elevate to levels they never thought possible. And certainly a task so great leaves miles to go before you sleep. Don't suppress the inspiration to lift. At the end of your career and your life, it will likely be the things you didn't get around to doing that you will regret more than the things you did.

Two More Astounding Examples

Example 1

In everything she did, in everything she stood for, Mother Teresa may have accomplished more than any mere mortal to promote dignity, honor, love and to rescue the poorest and most destitute on the planet. She not only lived the Leadership Revolution, but in so many ways, she embodied it.

For many, the winning of something as prestigious as the Nobel Peace Prize in 1979, as Mother Teresa did, would have been the highlight of one's existence. But not for this Albanian born nun who forsook a life of relative comfort to devote herself solely to serving the poor and forgotten.

The Process of Becoming: In 1946, Sister Teresa was working as a teacher at a small Catholic school in India. Like so many great leaders, her experiences led her to become one who was ready for a higher calling, a new way of thinking, or, in this case, undertaking what seemed to be the impossible.

On September 10th of that year, Mother Teresa had an experience that changed her life and ultimately changed the world. She felt a strong impression from God that she was to leave her convent school and serve the poor while living among them. In her own words, this wasn't an idealistic thought, but "an order." She took two years to prepare herself for what she thought might be the challenges she would face, including basic medical training, then turned in her nun's uniform for a simple white cotton sari with blue borders, a simple uniform that would come to be associated with her and her followers, the Missionaries of Charity, for nearly fifty years, continuing to this day.

Like so many leaders, she worked alone, for a long time, developing her vision and living her passion without fanfare and without external reward. Some, who heard of the work of this lonely nun, thought she was crazy. Perhaps this is what prompted her to state, "No matter who says what, you should accept it with a smile and do your own work." She was called and she knew it. To her it didn't matter who else knew it. She knew the work she was to lead. Did that mean she was sure of herself and the success of her daunting mission every step of the way? Of course not, but that isn't a requirement of a Revolutionary leader. Though tempted to return back to her "normal" life, she pressed on, full of conviction, love and a determination to fulfill her personal mission. She became one with the people she served. One in heart, one in soul.

The Process of Empowerment: In early 1949 her first followers joined her ranks. They came with no money, no corporate backing, just a desire to be empowered by the woman who had forsaken all, and in turn to empower those she loved. With no funding, they were forced to beg on the street for food and supplies. This was their and Mother Teresa's path to true empathy, understanding and experiencing the heartache and poverty of the poor. Mother Teresa reflected in her diary: "I thought how much they must ache in body and soul, looking for a home, food and health." Through diligence and determination, she was able to secure her first building from the local authorities, a former pilgrim hostel to use as her headquarters and the springboard for her newly empowered followers to use in continuing the work.

In those first few lonely years, with a new but faithful band of followers and a seemingly insurmountable task at hand, Mother Teresa demonstrated what it means to become and to empower with a belief in her vision, the toughness to never give up and a continued commitment to those around her. She showed compassion to the poor and those serving the poor, leading by example and empowering everyone in her wake to believe in themselves and believe in the impossible. She led by example in a life consuming desire to give everything she had to others.

The Process of Uniting: Come 1950, her following had grown substantially and she gained approval from the Pope to establish her efforts as a diocesan congregation, uniting her different ventures and increasingly international following under the mission of caring for "the hungry, the naked, the homeless, the crippled, the blind, the lepers, all those people who feel unwanted, unloved, uncared for throughout society, people that have become a burden to society and are shunned by everyone." Two years later she opened her first hospice for the dying poor in Kolkata, affectionately called Nirmal Hriday ("Home of the Pure Hearted"). The standard she had set in ministering to the destitute and sick, focusing on the dignity of the human being, was the unifying mission behind her organization's actions. In the hospice, religion was irrelevant as a condition for love, Christians, Muslims and Hindus we all given access to their own rites. In her own words, the home was for "people who [had] lived like animals to die like angels- loved and wanted."

The Process of Elevating: The Missionaries of Charity continued to grow, elevating to new heights in their vision of what could be accomplished and higher in their capacity to do good. Mother Teresa elevated her efforts as well, pursuing new ventures that supported her divine mission. She opened a leper house, Shanti Nagar (Place of Peace) as well as numerous clinics for leprosy. She opened a children's home she named Nirmala Shishu (Immaculate Heart Children's Home). Seeing the need to take her message and her mission farther than the streets of Kolkata, Mother Teresa expanded her reach and the Missionaries of Charity to other regions in India, and then across the world, opening homes in Africa, the United States and Europe.

In Elevating others, she taught profound truths, truths that will transform the lives of any woman or man seeking to give something more in life, leadership or legacy. See what principles you can find that recognize the Leadership Revolution.

"Spread love everywhere you go. Let no one ever come to you without leaving happier."

"We think sometimes that poverty is only being hungry, naked and homeless. The poverty of being unloved, unwanted and uncared for is the greatest poverty. We must start in our own homes to remedy this kind of poverty."

"Be faithful in small things because it is in them that your strength lies."

"If you can't feed a hundred people, then feed just one."

"If we have no peace it is because we have forgotten that we belong to each other."

"The miracle is not that we do this work, it is that we are happy to do it."

"The hunger for love is much more difficult to remove than the hunger for bread."

"Kind words can be short and easy to speak, but their echoes are truly endless."

The Leadership Revolution Continued: Mother Teresa continued to grow, continued to become, empowered thousands, if not millions with her example, united across global boundaries and elevated all that was good, again and again and again. That kind of elevation inspired even Pope John Paul II himself, who, while visiting Kolkata, claimed that Teresa's efforts bore witness of the "primacy of love." Upon her death nearly twenty years later, this same Pope stated, who himself was the leader of over 1 billion followers, "I am personally grateful to this courageous woman who I have always felt beside me... Her life is a testimony to the dignity and privilege of human dignity and humble service." At that same time, the former United Nations Secretary General from Peru, Javier Perez de Cuellar stated, "She is the United Nations. She is Peace to the world." Mother Teresa too humble and consumed in others would likely have never said that of herself, even though she was known to be fluent in five languages herself, but she did on one occasion remark, "By blood I am Albanian. By citizenship am Indian. By faith, I am a Catholic nun. As to my calling, I belong to the world. As to my heart, I belong entirely to the Heart of Jesus."

Mother Teresa continued to elevate, higher and higher on the spiral staircase known as the Leadership Revolution. Her teachings have altered lives, communities and even the policies of countries. What started as one determined woman working alone on the streets of India in 1948 became a group of 14 just a year later. By 1997 the Missionaries of Charity grew to over 4,000 sisters with a partnering male order of over 300 brothers. The Missionaries of Charity started on just a couple of streets in Kolkata, but today are active in over 310 countries around the world.

Example 2

The Disney Company: No one would have thought when the Disney Brothers Cartoon Studio opened its doors in 1923 that it would one day it would grow to be the greatest influence on family media the world had ever seen. Well, maybe the brothers themselves saw it, and that's all that really mattered at first.

The Process of Becoming: Walt Disney, who became the face as well as the heart of the brothers' company, was no stranger to hard work. After serving a year in France in the post-World War I Red Cross, Disney took his artistic talents and began to put them to use in a series of companies he founded in the Midwest. A short time later, each of these companies failed despite his drive and passion. Undeterred, Walt took the lessons he learned, stuck to his guns and moved to California. Not content with working for someone else and repeating a mistake he had previously made of letting another own his creativity, the Disney Company, as it's known today, took control of its destiny with nothing more than imagination and lessons learned through minor successes and overwhelming failure. Failure that Walt chose not to fear. In this process of becoming, it was Disney who said, 'All our dreams can come true, if we have the courage to pursue them."

Walt's own dreams kept the company pushing the boundaries of innovation in entertainment. Mickey Mouse was born with a soul of his own, followed by his friends, Donald Duck, Goofy and Pluto. The movies then started changing the world, with Snow White, Cinderella and Bambi joining the fold. The success only multiplied in the years to come and it was at this time that Walt could have easily called it a day, hung up his hat, and spent the rest of his days in luxury. He could have lived out his life confident he had become one of the great leaders of the century. But he had another dream to accomplish.

The Process of Empowering: What started as a simple sketch on a business trip, eventually became the blueprint for Disneyland. The skeptics predicted the park would fail, Disney didn't care. He proceeded with confidence. Walt knew he couldn't build something this monumental on his own. He needed the buy in and skill of those who shared his vision. Enter Doug Lipp's fascinating work on the emergence of the University of Disneyland, now known as Disney University, and the inspired work of Van France, the trainer and visionary who would make Disney's dream a reality, even after Walt himself left the earth.

Van France was given short and to the point instructions by Disney. "Help me create the "Happiest Place on Earth." France, empowered with the confidence of an inspiring leader set out to do just that and became an ever inspiring leader himself. "Armed with a clear vision and leadership support and surrounded by an immensely talented team, Van France created an institution that continues to define excellence and unparalleled success." It was said that it was his university that became the catalyst of the Disney Magic.

This was no easy task. It was France who was credited with taking the complexity of everything Disney stood for and empowering others to feel they were a part of Disney's vision and that Disney's vision was a part of them. As Lipp, a trainer at the University himself, wrote, "We take care of the cast, the cast takes care of our guests and our business thrives." It all began and still begins with empowering every employee to internalize the timeless vision of bringing happiness to every guest, every day.

The Process of Uniting: Walt Disney himself stated the challenges that laid beyond the spectacular buildings and innovative attractions of his new "Magical Kingdom". "We need to mold a group of diverse Californians, with no business experience, into producers of the "Disneyland Dream." How did France accomplish such a feat? By uniting his team of "cast members" behind Disney's vision and the Disneyland experience. "Disneyland is the star, everything else is in the supporting role."

France emphasized priorities. "What happens 'backstage' will end up 'on stage.' If we aren't friendly with each other... smiling and saying 'good morning' and things like that, then we'll have a similar attitude towards our guests." Everything was about "the show", everything was about "the vision", and everything was about "the guest". EVERYTHING. France made it easy for the cast members to unite on an intellectual and an emotional level, a skill desired by every leader, but possessed by few.

The Process of Elevating: The goal was that Disneyland would never be "completed" and that it would always continue to new heights in customer service and new levels of imagination. In a memorandum from 1962, France wrote, "Disneyland will never be completed. We've certainly lived up to that promise. But what about the people that operate it? Are we growing with the show or just getting older? The trouble with people is that we get hardening of the mental arteries, cirrhosis of the enthusiasm, and arthritis of the imagination, along with chronic and sometimes acute allergies to supervision, subordinates, the whole darned system. Is it possible that what we have gained through experience, we have lost through habit, and that what we have gained through organization, we have lost in enthusiasm?"

No one understood the necessity of elevating the organization and the organizational member better than Van France. He showed the way in everything he did for the Disney Corporation. Behind four guiding principles he mentored and elevated a generation of Disney employees; Innovation, Organizational Support, Education and Entertainment. These four principles ensured the Disneyland dream for decades and ensures it today throughout all its parks and its numerous resorts.

The Leadership Revolution Continued: Both Disney and France saw the vision, lived the vision and communicated the vision. The legacy is apparent as the company continues to unite together and change the world through the power of imagination. In the words of Disney, "Why do we have to grow up? That's the real trouble with the world, too many people grow up. They forget. They don't remember what it's like to be twelve years old." Disney felt that "growing up" was the equivalent of losing joy in your work, a passion in your creativity and that drive to innovate. This was never the case under Disney and France, and after a half a century dedicated to a culture driven by the Leadership Revolution, it's not likely to happen any time soon.

CONCLUSION

Belief

The Leadership Revolution will never work unless you believe with all your heart that you can elevate continually. Belief is the power that will keep you motivated, keep you excited, keep you moving when the steps get steep. If you believe you can succeed and want to succeed bad enough, the tools in this book will guarantee your success. The Leadership Revolution is only as powerful as a process as it is mastered in your mind! What you think will determine your reality! Confucius made a profound point, "The will to win, the desire to succeed, the urge to reach your full potential... these are the keys that will unlock the door to personal excellence." We would add organizational excellence as well.

Your belief is the catalyst for the belief of those around you. Throughout history it has been the leader's most crucial responsibility to instill belief in others. Let's work through several deep seated examples.

Winston Churchill: The Last Lion, Winston Churchill became prime minister of the British empire during the rage and toil of World War II. Three days after taking office he met with his cabinet and said the following, "I have nothing to offer but blood, toil, tears and sweat." He lived up to that statement. With the Axis Army storming through West through Europe towards the British Isles, Churchill delivered one of the most famous speeches in history that inspired belief in a time where little was to be found.

"I have, myself, full confidence that if all do their duty, if nothing is neglected, and if the best arrangements are made, as they are being made, we shall prove ourselves once again able to defend our Island home, to ride out the storm of war, and to outlive the menace of tyranny, if necessary for years, if necessary alone. At any rate, that is what we are going to try to do. That is the resolve of His Majesty's Government-every man of them. That is the will of Parliament and the nation. The British Empire and the French Republic, linked together in their cause and in their need, will defend to the death their native soil, aiding each other like good comrades to the utmost of their strength. Even though large tracts of Europe and many old and famous States have fallen or may fall into the grip of the Gestapo and all the odious apparatus of Nazi rule, we shall not flag or fail. We shall go on to the end, we shall fight in France, we shall fight on the seas and oceans, we shall fight with growing confidence and growing strength in the air, we shall defend our Island, whatever the cost may be, we shall fight on the beaches, we shall fight on the landing grounds, we shall fight in the fields and in the streets, we shall fight in the hills; we shall never surrender, and even if, which I do not for a moment believe, this Island or a large part of it were subjugated and starving, then our Empire beyond the seas, armed and guarded by the British Fleet, would carry on the struggle, until, in God's good time, the New World, with all its power and might, steps forth to the rescue and the liberation of the old."

Susan B Anthony was a women's rights activist arrested for casting a vote in the presidential election. Her courage and belief inspired thousands. The following speech was no exception.

Friends and Fellow Citizens: I stand before you tonight under indictment for the alleged crime of having voted at the last presidential election, without having a lawful right to vote. It shall be my work this evening to prove to you that in thus voting, I not only committed no crime, but, instead, simply exercised my citizen's rights, guaranteed to me and all United States citizens by the National Constitution, beyond the power of any State to deny.

The preamble of the Federal Constitution says:

"We, the people of the United States, in order to form a more perfect union, establish justice, insure domestic tranquility, provide for the common defense, promote the general welfare, and secure the blessings of liberty to ourselves and our posterity, do ordain and establish this Constitution for the United States of America."

It was we, the people; not we, the white male citizens; nor yet we, the male citizens; but we, the whole people, who formed the Union. And we formed it, not to give the blessings of liberty, but to secure them; not to the half of ourselves and the half of our posterity, but to the whole people--women as well as men. And it is a downright mockery to talk to women of their enjoyment of the blessings of liberty while they are denied the use of the only means of securing them provided by this democratic-republican government--the ballot.

For any State to make sex a qualification that must ever result in the disfranchisement of one entire half of the people is to pass a bill of attainder, or an ex post facto law, and is therefore a violation of the supreme law of the land. By it the blessings of liberty are forever withheld from women and their female posterity. To them this government has no just powers derived from the consent of the governed. To them this government is not a democracy. It is not a republic. It is an odious aristocracy; a hateful oligarchy of sex; the most hateful aristocracy ever established on the face of the globe; an oligarchy of wealth, where the right govern the poor. An oligarchy of learning, where the educated govern the ignorant, or even an oligarchy of race, where the Saxon rules the African, might be endured; but this oligarchy of sex, which makes father, brothers, husband, sons, the oligarchs over the mother and sisters, the wife and daughters of every household--which ordains all men sovereigns, all women subjects, carries dissension, discord and rebellion into every home of the nation.

Webster, Worcester and Bouvier all define a citizen to be a person in the United States, entitled to vote and hold office.

The only question left to be settled now is: Are women persons? And I hardly believe any of our opponents will have the hardihood to say they are not. Being persons, then, women are citizens; and no State has a right to make any law, or to enforce any old law, that shall abridge their privileges or immunities.

Abraham Lincoln: As we discussed previously, Lincoln faced with pressure few leaders have ever known, and in light of the bloodiest conflict in the history of the United States, President Lincoln understood that belied in a common purpose was the only thing that could unite the union. His belief he could and would succeed was powerful and contagious. He was quoted as saying, "Always bear in mind that your own resolution to succeed is more important than any other." Ultimately, and with great sacrifice, they did succeed in preserving the union. The Gettysburg address, delivered on the battlefield of the most crucial importance in the American Civil War was a powerful reflection of Lincoln's belief.

Four score and seven years ago our fathers brought forth on this continent, a new nation, conceived in Liberty, and dedicated to the proposition that all men are created equal.

The Allazo Group

Now we are engaged in a great civil war, testing whether that nation, or any nation so conceived and so dedicated, can long endure. We are met on a great battlefield of that war. We have come to dedicate a portion of that field, as a final resting place for those who here gave their lives that that nation might live. It is altogether fitting and proper that we should do this.

But, in a larger sense, we cannot dedicate -- we cannot consecrate -- we cannot hallow -- this ground. The brave men, living and dead, who struggled here, have consecrated it, far above our poor power to add or detract. The world will little note, nor long remember what we say here, but it can never forget what they did here. It is for us the living, rather, to be dedicated here to the unfinished work which they who fought here have thus far so nobly advanced. It is rather for us to be here dedicated to the great task remaining before us -- that from these honored dead we take increased devotion to that cause for which they gave the last full measure of devotion -- that we here highly resolve that these dead shall not have died in vain -- that this nation, under God, shall have a new birth of freedom -- and that government of the people, by the people, for the people, shall not perish from the earth.

These leader's words were only matched by their actions. Their belief showed itself in lives dedicated to far more than their own. Is this not leadership? No, it is the very definition of the Leadership Revolution; to progress high enough on those trying, cycling stairs to the point where we realize that our leadership was never ours alone, but shared with those who showed us the way and our opportunity to do the same for others. And thus the Revolution continues, onward and upward, generation by generation.

How You Know the Cycle is Working

Being able to measure the results of your efforts is key in not only in the Leadership Revolution but in every organizational endeavor. So how do you know the Leadership Revolution is working for you personally and for your organization? Fill out the following charts, be honest with yourself and it should give you an excellent idea of where you currently stand. You can begin this chart now and update it six months.

QUESTION	Where were you when you started applying the revolution principles?	Where are you now?
How engaged are your employees?		
How many people in your organization consider themselves leaders?		
How United is your team?		
How many in your organization have personal progress plans?		
How much time are you spending coaching others?		

How effective is your organization in goal setting?		
What level of commitment is their organization wide to your team's purpose and mission?		

What percentage of YOUR time is spent in the following areas out of a total of 100 points?

Dealing with Conflict	Empowering Others	Trying to Unite a Team
Presiding over a United Team	Innovating with those you lead	Struggling to make bottom line progress

Planning for the Future

Planning for the future has a great deal to do with seeing a purpose, a vision and goal setting. But how can we start? With three profound questions that can be asked over and over again. Fill out the answers to these questions below, as they apply to you.

What are three things we are currently doing as an organization, or am I doing as an individual, that are keeping the organization from progressing, that need to stop today?

_____

_____

_____

_____

_____

_____

_____

_____

_____

_____

_____

_____

_____

_____

_____

_____

The Allazo Group

What are three things that either I or the organization need to keep doing in order to progress in the Leadership Revolution?

_____

_____

_____

_____

_____

_____

_____

_____

_____

_____

_____

_____

_____

_____

_____

_____

_____

What are three things, either I or the organization as a whole can start doing today to further ourselves in the Leadership Revolution?

_____

_____

_____

_____

_____

_____

_____

_____

_____

_____

_____

_____

_____

_____

_____

_____

_____

_____

_____

Our Journey from Here

As we said in the beginning, there are thousands of leadership books out there. But here's the thing, you can take any two books and chances are they are going to contradict each other. Even books based on "cutting edge research" battle the same issue with differing, even opposite opinions on what makes a good and even great leader. So what is the aspiring leader within you supposed to do?

The key is not in seeking direct answers or quick fixes in your developmental progression, as if one cliché statement could be the catalyst you desire. Instead, here is how we view the issue. It is best to look at leadership principles as just that, principles, not absolutes. They are guide posts. One thing may apply to your situation perfectly while another will be as effective as trying to fit a square into a round hole. But when you understand the principles inside and out, you can easily navigate the course that best fits you, your team and your current state of leadership.

The Leadership Revolution is meant to provide the fundamental principles you can apply to your specific situation, whatever it may be. At the heart of great leadership, these four principles have always existed. Use them to build, empower, unite and elevate everyone within your reach.

Some say the journey of a thousand miles starts with one step. You already took that step a long time ago, even the first time you looked inwards and asked yourself, "How can I be better?" Many infer there is a promise land at some point of arrival, we would contend that the greatest gifts a leader can give and receive are the lessons found in the journey, one revolution of ascension at a time.

ABOUT THE ALLAZO GROUP

The Allazo Group is a global consulting company dedicated to educating for empowerment. Visit us at www.Allazogroup.com for more information about the authors, other publications, classes and resources to help you reach your full potential.

ABOUT THE AUTHORS

Lead Author - Scott Catt

Scott Catt is a co-founder and partner at The Allazo Group. Born and raised in Tucson, Arizona, Scott is a graduate of Brigham Young University and did his masters work in Organizational Behavior at the University of London and Cambridge University. Through the course of his studies Scott has focused his attentions on leadership as seen throughout history and has sought to bridge the gap between the styles and strategies of great leaders in the past and principle based application in the modern worlds of education and business. A passionate educator, Scott has led over forty teachers and over thirty administrators in several educational institutions and as a business professional has served as a Vice President and Senior Vice President at several national and international companies as well as a director at one of the world's most prestigious consulting firms. He is fluent in Spanish and has diverse experience working with peoples and organizations from

North and South America, Africa and Europe. A prolific speaker, he has presented and trained at a wide variety of events and conferences. Scott is a friend to all and looks forward to meeting you at your next event.

Supporting Author - Scott Coleman

Scott is a Utah native, a Sugar Bowl Champion and a friend of youth. A co-founder of The Allazo Group, Scott inspires companies and employees to reach their full potential.

Supporting Author - Clark Bateman

Clark is a Texan, a thought leader in the marketing world and an enthusiast of all things Spain. He co-founded The Allazo Group with Scott Catt and Scott Coleman and is a driving force behind making the group's dreams, realities.